Daniel Lord

The Effect of Secession Upon the Commercial Relations

Between the North and South, and Upon Each Section

Daniel Lord

The Effect of Secession Upon the Commercial Relations
Between the North and South, and Upon Each Section

ISBN/EAN: 9783337253721

Printed in Europe, USA, Canada, Australia, Japan

Cover: Foto ©ninafisch / pixelio.de

More available books at **www.hansebooks.com**

THE EFFECT

OF

SECESSION

UPON THE

COMMERCIAL RELATIONS

BETWEEN THE

NORTH AND SOUTH,

AND UPON

EACH SECTION.

NEW YORK:

OFFICE OF THE NEW YORK TIMES,

PRINTING HOUSE SQUARE.

1861.

The articles on the following pages are reprints from the NEW YORK TIMES, with such changes as were necessary to adapt them to a different style of publication.

History of American Economy: Studies and Materials for Study
A series of reprints of the important studies
and source books relating to the growth of the
American economic system.

General Editor: William N. Parker

First reprinting, 1966, Johnson Reprint Corporation

Printed in the United States of America

SECESSION:

ITS EFFECT UPON THE COMMERCIAL RELA-
TIONS BETWEEN THE NORTH AND
SOUTH, AND UPON EACH
SECTION.

THE postulate from which we start is Secession. The possibility of such an event is assumed for the purpose of meas-
uring the effect upon the commercial relations between the
North and South, and upon each section, of the most extreme
measures threatened. The subject will be discussed purely in
its material aspects and consequences ; those of a moral or
political character being referred to only when too intimately
connected with the former to be readily separated therefrom.

MOTIVES TO SECESSION ON THE PART OF THE SOUTH.

The leading motive or inducement to Secession has un-
doubtedly been the anticipated material advantages that were
to result. For nearly half a century South Carolina, the
author of the movement, has been dissatisfied with the policy
of the General Government as to the mode of raising its
revenues. In 1832, this dissatisfaction very nearly broke out

in open rebellion, but was awed into submission by the determined attitude of General Jackson, then President of the
United States; but, the question was not settled—only post-
poned by the adoption of the compromise of Mr. Clay. It
was the doctrine of Mr. Calhoun and Mr. McDuffie, sub-
scribed to by the people of their State, and by a large party
throughout the South, that the operations of the General
Government were most oppressive to a section which, according to their views, supplied, indirectly to be sure, the larger
portion of its revenues, to be expended almost entirely in the
Northern States, stimulating their progress in wealth and
population to an extraordinary degree, and paralyzing in an
equal degree that of the South. While every year that section sent abroad products varying from one to two hundred
millions of dollars in value, only one-tenth the amount was
returned to them in direct importations. The balance disap-
peared, they could hardly tell how. But as all their exports
went into the hands of the " Yankee," who monopolized the
carrying trade, the inference to their minds became irresistible
that by some trick of cunning or smartness, or by partial
legislation, he contrived to appropriate a large portion of them
to his own use. By means of the wealth wrested in this
manner from the South, the commerce, trade, manufactures,
and wealth of the North constantly expanded, acquiring col-
lossal proportions, while those of the South either remained
stationary or dwindled into insignificance. Each year only
served to render the contrast more striking. A system, or
Government, the operations of which, as they assumed,
produced such results, could not fail to become in
time, objects of dislike and aversion. This feeling was
greatly aggravated by false and extravagant notions
which prevailed in the Southern States as to the power
they possessed in monetary and commercial affairs, by virtue
of their great staple—*Cotton*. The consumption of this
article had increased with a rapidity unprecedented in the
annals of domestic economy. It had come to be of common
use in every family in Christendom. In England millions

were employed in its manufacture, the support of whom, if not their very existence, depended upon a steady supply of this staple. In the foreign commerce of this country it had come to be the leading figure, reaching $191,000,000 in value the past year—a sum equaling nearly one half the total exports of the country. It was felt to be unendurable, that a people, possessing a monopoly of the production of an article upon which millions depended for existence in the leading commercial country of the world, and upon which the foreign trade of our own was largely based, should be the subject of an oppression by our Government, so excessive as to destroy their commercial and manufacturing development, to check their population, and hold them in a position of degrading vassalage. At the same time they believed that neither England nor France would allow our own Government to take any steps that would interfere with the production or free movement of cotton, but would resist the same to the full extent of their power, even to the declaration of war against it. This feeling was still further stimulated by the importance to which the wealth and power of the South were magnified by interested parties, and the numerous crowd who paid them court. The Southern people were taught to believe they held in their hand the destinies of the world; that to withhold their cotton would bankrupt England, France, and all the Northern States. They were so often reminded of their power, that in the absence of any well defined notions of Political Economy, they were raised to a state of mental ecstasy, which had about as little relation to common sense, or to ordinary affairs, as the fancies of Don Quixote.

As an illustration of the condition of the Southern mind, under the influences described, we copy the following article from *De Bow's Southern Review*, for January, written by Major W. H. Chase, of Pensacola, Florida, one of the most respectable and widely-known gentlemen in the Southern country which presents the whole *animus* on which secession is based and expresses with entire fidelity and accuracy the Southern view of the movement, its desirableness and commercial advantages, and the complete impunity and protection with which it is to be accomplished :

"SOUTHERN SECESSION—ITS STATUS AND ADVANTAGES.

" The secession of these States' must necessarily be a *peaceful one*, because England, France, and the rest of commercial Europe, and the Western and North-Western States of the Union, require that it should be.

" The programme of secession would be inaugurated by proceedings deliberate, dignified and determined.

" This great revolution would be duly announced in advance of the overt act, so that England and France especially, and the Western States, should be made acquainted with its nature, and with the great *commercial benefits* that would result to them by its development.

" The nature of the revolution would be due to a *radical change in the political and commercial relations of the seceding States with the commercial world, at home and abroad ;* by which a free market would be opened to general commerce ; by which the great West would be relieved of duties ranging up to thirty per cent. on foreign articles consumed by its inhabitants ; and by which their great staples would flow freely through the rivers and railways of Southern ports and sections ; and there, in combination with the cotton, sugar, rice and tobacco of those sections, form the basis of exchanges with the world.

" The benefits to be derived to the commercial nations at home and abroad, would be : First, the products of the great West, as well as of the South, whose chief interests lie in agriculture, would be transported to the home and foreign markets at cheaper rates than many of them now are, because the lines of railways to the Southern ports would transport freight every day in the year, unimpeded by the snow of winter ; and, second, the foreign ships, being placed under free trade principles, would so powerfully compete with the Northern ships as to reduce freights from its Southern ports to the lowest living rates. England and France, thus stimulated, would especially increase their steam commercial marine ; and, in a very short time, relieved of the great burdens now imposed in discriminating duties by the Government of the Union, *they would become the chief carriers of American products and supplies.* Their ships would come loaded with the products of every nation, and, delivering them at Norfolk,

Charleston, Savannah, Fernandina, Pensacola, Mobile and New Orleans, would be reloaded with the rich products of the South and West. In less than six months from this time, every one of the above ports will have been connected directly by railways with the valleys of the Mississippi and Missouri, and with the vast regions lying to the north, the south, the east and the west. Nor are these facilities of intercommunication of the South with the West necessary to be mentioned in order to demonstrate the great political and commercial advantages which would be due to the secession of the Cotton States, and which would be enjoyed by them and all countries trading with them.

" Demonstrations already made, so patent to the mind of the statesman, viewing them either in their political and commercial, or in their national and international aspects, will be keenly perceived and vigilantly observed, as their resultants are disclosed. And so important—almost vitally so—will they be to the interests of the observers, that the men of the West and the East *will pause in their threatened hostility to the revolution, while England and France would send powerful fleets to insure its peaceful maintenance.* The men of the West would not only instantly pause in any hostile course to it, *but they would demand that their great section should be united politically,* as it would be commercially, to the new Confederacy. In this movement they would be joined by such of the Slave States as had kept aloof from the first movement of secession. And thus that great movement would lead directly, and in a brief time, to a more perfect union among *twenty-four States*— leaving the *shipping State* of Maine, and the commercial and manufacturing States of Massachusetts, Vermont, New Hampshire, Connecticut, Rhode Island, New Jersey and Pennsylvania to work out their salvation in their own way. They would have a clear field to work in, for their present basis of trade, navigation and manufactures, *would have been entirely swept away.* Indeed, all the great and glorious material prosperity they now enjoy, and so much boast of, would become 'as the baseless fabric of a vision—leaving not a wreck behind.'

" The first demonstration of blockade of the Southern ports would be swept away by the *English fleets of observation hovering on the Southern coasts,* to protect English commerce, and especially the free flow of Cotton to English and French factories. The flow of Cotton must not cease for a day : because the enormous sum of £150,000,000 is annually due to the elaboration of raw Cotton · and because 5,000,000 of people derive their daily and immediate support therefrom in England alone, and every interest throughout the kingdom is connected therewith.

"Nor must the Cotton States be invaded by land, for it would interrupt the cultivation of the great staple. The great cotton zone of the world must never cease to be cultivated; the plow and the hoe, and the cotton gin must never cease to move; but war and invasion would tend to that result, or at least create dangerous obstruction to cultivation. *Invaders, then, would have to be restrained by force.* And whence would that force be derived? From what has already been briefly considered, the answer is easily framed. *The force would be derived from the West,* whose interests lie in the free ports and free markets of the South. *The force would be derived from England and France,* whose interests are deeply concerned in maintaining an uninterrupted supply of Cotton; in the free trade of the Southern and Western countries, and in the carrying trade of their great products; and the force would be derived from Kentucky, Tennessee, North Carolina, and Virginia—the frontier Slave States through which Northern people would not be permitted to pass; *and if they were, England would check that movement by blockading New York, Boston, &c.*

"Assuming the revolution to be *un fait accompli*—a thing in its fulfilment complete within itself, and its fulfillers actuated by no desire to take one step backwards in the process—the question will again be asked, what will be the *status* of the Slave or Cotton States in their sovereign and independent condition? And it will be answered, that it will be that which is due to the inherent power of dependence, and the prosperity due to the possession of the *cotton zone* of the world; and it may again be further answered, that this power and prosperity will be, and, indeed is, *triply fortified and maintained by the entire power of England, France,* and the commercial world, whose interests, almost vitally so, depend upon the production of millions of bales of cotton in the Slave States; while the prosperity of these leading nations would be greatly enhanced by the free markets and free ships which the declaration of free trade would open to them. And while these things were enacted with a celerity due to the advantages to be reaped by these agricultural States, an *exodus,* unexampled in the world's movement, either of traditionary or historical times, *would pour forth from the dark and fanatical regions of the North into the smiling regions of the South and West.* The migration from Europe, under the influence of free trade, and the increasing demands for American production, would produce a movement

in that direction far surpassing any known in the history of
European exodus into America. Thus, population, with its attendant wealth and power, would be stimulated and increased;
and through such an example, the neighboriug States, Provinces and Colonies throughout the North American Continent,
would be urged to assume the same *status*. The fanatical
demagogues of the North and Middle States would be de-
prived of power by an indignant and ruined people ; but the
States, with energies and intellect awakened by the severe
ordeal to which a dissolution of the Union will have subjected
them, would either claim to be admitted into the new Confederacy of Free Trade States, or, in their independent condition,
endeavor to recover their losses in some degree by the adoption of free trade principles. To this political and commercial
condition Canada and the British Provinces must come at last ;
and to this condition Cuba and Mexico would most willingly
assimilate, either by annexation to the Southern and Western
Confederacy, or by the practice of free trade principles as
sovereign and independent nations.

" Under the movements, and through their attendant wealth
and power, the completion of the great lines of communication, and the commencement of new ones, would connect the
valleys of the Mississippi, Missouri, Red River, the Rio
Grande, and the magnificent valleys of Mexico with New Orleans, Mobile, Pensacola, Apalachicola, St. Marks, Key West,
Fernandina, Savannah, Charleston and Norfolk. Under these
influences, the values of property would be enhanced, and yet
not to a degree so as to discourage any one from efforts to
possess it. While the aggregate value of the lands in the
South or West would be greatly increased, there would be
millions of acres held within our wide domain at prices that
any industrious man could give. For, great as the influx of
laborers and cultivators would be to our Southern and Western fields, yet the ' further Ind ' would unfold its rich soil to
their enterprise and industry.

" A confederacy possessing such elements of wealth, prosperity and power, would possess all the elements of peace at
home, and the means, under a wise and just Government, of
preserving it with foreign nations ; because, producing natur-
ally what those countries wanted, and could not do without,
and requiring what they produced in manufactures and handi-
craft, they would, as it has already been shown, *remain in sympathy with the new Confederacy*. Hence, no armies or navies
would be required to preserve either national or international
relations ; neither these, nor a host of office-holders due to the

collection of revenue of a high tariff, would be necessary to the maintenance of the Government of the Confederacy. In short, the annual expenditures for the same need not, for all efficient purposes, *exceed those now due to one of the large States of the Union.*"

Here is a true picture of the Southern mind. It shows us with what we have to deal, and explains the conduct of the people of the Cotton States so incomprehensible and incredible to those of the North.

HOW THE SOUTH GOT THEIR MISTAKEN NOTIONS.

Everything is easy and plain to him who never accomplished anything, simply because he has no notion of the cost of anything *well* done. He consequently assumes in his favor the best of whatever other people do. The South see the North possessed of ships, commerce, manufactures, wealth and population, but they do not see the method by which these have been created. They imagine all these things *happened* at the North by being desired, and will come to them the same way, or by change in *political* relations; that they can be *improvised* by resolutions passed at political and social gatherings. Such resolutions for thirty years past have annually declared that they *ought* and *should* become a great manufacturing and commercial people. But no one had the disposition, personally, to undergo the sacrifice and training necessary to such a result. In fact, they could not feel or understand the necessity of such sacrifice or training. Without the corrections and limitations of experience, their imaginations ran wild as to their fancied capabilities and power. They lent a willing ear to the most extravagant statements and schemes which assumed to teach them how to rival the North. To them the creation of a city like New York, on their own soil, was mere child's play. As it is as easy to wish for a great as a little thing, they went the whole figure, and are firmly convinced that a destiny as big as their imaginations awaits them, nothing daunted by the complete failure, thus far, of all their dreams. and resolutions.

The remedy for all such fancies is experience. The Seceding States must now make good their assumptions or submit to a disastrous defeat. They must immediately take steps that will test their means and strength, and must as certainly fail, unless they prove ignorance to be stronger than skill ; inexperience than training ; that aptitudes go for nothing, and that labor held in dishonor is more productive than that held in respect—in fact, unless the whole order of things is reversed, and success is to come from being desired instead of being earned.

THE COTTON STATES MUST CONTINUE TO PUSH THE PRODUCTION OF THEIR STAPLE TO THE FULL EXTENT OF THEIR MEANS.

The South must continue to produce. Cotton, not only as a means of existence, but because they can put their labor to no other use. According to their estimate, they have $4,000,000,000 invested in labor, chiefly engaged in the culture of this staple. The interest, at 6 per cent., on this sum is $240,000,000. If there were no other motive, they are not going to let this vast investment lie idle. As soon would the owner of a cotton mill in Lowell stop work because he had taken a miff at parties who are accustomed to purchase or transport his fabrics. On the contrary, the Southern planter will, under all circumstances, push the culture of the staple to the utmost extent. For this we have the strongest of all guarantees—cupidity and the instinct of self-preservation. He must raise cotton or starve. If he raises it in sufficient quantities to buy food, he will in sufficient quantities to buy clothing, the comforts and luxuries of life, and to render his investment profitable. The planter will not prove, in the long run, a fool, nor a person much differing from the rest of mankind, however great may be his present folly. He will overstock the market at all times if he can. He has not been able to do so for some time past, on account of the rapidly increasing demand. No one has any fear that he will not do his best to raise a crop, or sell it when raised; but there are fears that it may fail from drought, or a blight, or negro insurrections, or war.   Once raised, it will go to the consumer with as much certainty as water runs down hill.   It is to avoid some of the contingencies to the crop, that efforts are everywhere making to raise a supply elsewhere.

WHAT ARE THE REAL RELATIONS BETWEEN THE NORTH AND SOUTH, AND ON WHAT ARE THEY BASED.

The commercial relations between the North and South are based on natural laws, and are entirely distinct from, and independent of political ones.   The South produces certain articles necessary to commerce that cannot be raised North, while climate and other conditions enable the North to manufacture more cheaply and skilfully than at the South, and beget a spirit of maritime adventure which renders them the carriers for the whole country.   In certain products, from difference of climate, each excels, and must continue to excel the other.   The North cannot compete with the South in the culture of sugar or cotton.   But the fervid sun which these require, relaxes the muscles and indisposes to physical exertion.   The South, therefore, cannot compete with the North in manufactures and commerce, which require great physical and nervous energy, which is the product of temperate zones, which the sun, for a portion of the year, leaves to snow and ice.   The relations between the two sections are based on differences which can never be changed by human agency.

THE EFFECT OF SECESSION ON THE DIRECT TRADE BETWEEN THE SOUTH AND EUROPE.

One of the great advantages which the Cotton States pictures themselves as springing from Secession is *direct trade* with Europe.   The want of this has been for a long time most galling to their pride.   They produce one half of our exports to foreign countries. These are all taken away in *Northern* vessels, which bring back the proceeds, not to *Southern* but to *Northern* ports. They see that Northern cities rapidly expand in population, commerce, and wealth, while theirs remain stationary, or fall into decay. The diversion, as they term it, of this trade, they ascribe to the action of the National Government, which fosters enterprise at the North, and discourages it at the South. The destruction of this Government, consequently, is to free them from their thraldom, and return to them in gold, silver and merchandize, the $150,000,000 sent abroad in Cotton. They will thus change places with the North, make their ports the emporiums for the whole country, and compel the Northern people to come to them for their supplies of foreign merchandize.

In reasoning in this manner, the Southern people entirely overlook the evidence, drawn from experience, of their aptitudes and capabilities. The pursuits and development of both North and South are simply the unfolding of natural laws or tendencies. If the two sections differ in results, they must differ equally in cause. The Southern people do not become sailors, because they have no aptitudes for maritime pursuits. If they do not build ships proves either a lack of industry, or mechanical skill, or suitable materials, or good harbors, or a healthy climate. The South is wanting in all these particulars but materials. These, consequently, have to be sent North, where the people possess everything *but* material. No people with the climate, or sea-coast of the South, ever did, or ever can become maritime. Another obstacle is their social system. The forecastle is not to be trusted to a crew of slaves. The poor whites have no taste for the toil and subordination necessary to constitute good sailors. Were this fact otherwise, Southern ports are too liable to fatal epidemics to allow any development in industry, wealth or population, beyond that necessary to perform the *export* trade of the districts dependent upon them. Manufactures cannot flourish in them, because an interruption for a month in a year would prove fatal to their success. Charleston has no more population than it had ten years ago, for the reason that its export trade is but little greater. Another fatal obstacle to Southern cities becoming great depots of trade is that of climate, which is destructive to many kinds of merchandize if they remain long in store or warehouse. All Southern cities, consequently, are only points *in transitu* of merchandize on its way from the manufacturer or merchant, who must reside in a climate which favors the prosecution of their industries the year round, and the accumulation of their products till they can be sent, with profit, to the consumers.

The South, consequently, can no more compete with the North in maritime pursuits on equal terms, than the North with them in the production of Cotton. Success on either side must be in the direction of the natural advantages each possesses. As they cannot build or run ships, they cannot direct who shall carry their products. The party who will do it cheapest will always be preferred, no matter what his politics. When the planter sells his cotton on the wharf at Charleston, he parts with all power over its direction or mode of transit. He might as well direct who shall weave and wear it, or with equal reason declare who were to be the fortunate persons who were to transport tea from the Celestial Empire to *outside barbarians*. The absurdity of one assumption is not a whit more glaring than the other. We know that the South threaten to exclude Northern ships from their ports. All such threats are purely absurd. Such an act passed to-day would be repealed to-morrow. The people are not yet all fools, even in South Carolina; nor will they, any more than Yankeedom refuse a good bargain because driven with parties of different politics. Men may, in a moment of passion, make laws hostile to their interests, but when reason returns they will not be long in repealing them.

If the North are to carry the cotton to Europe, for the same reason they must *bring back the proceeds*. Such a result is inevitable. The bulk of freights going to Europe vastly exceeds that coming to the United States. As the returning ships average only half a cargo, we do not think Southern people are going to send ships out in *ballast*, for the sake of bringing them back half loaded, even to their own ports. But if they should attempt such an unheard of absurdity, their ships would have to bring their cargoes to Northern cities. Why? Because these, representing the North, own such cargoes, having paid for them in advances to the Southern people of what they consume. A mere fraction of our foreign imports finds its way to the Southern States. These States do not consume foreign but *domestic* merchandize. They import from the North ten dollars in domestics for every one imported, directly or indirectly, from Europe. If they opened a *direct* trade, they would not have returned to their ports more than a tenth, in value, of their exports. The balance would never enter their harbors in any contingency. It would go by the shortest route to the parties to whom it belonged. The construction and maintenance of a foreign commercial system, under which the return freight would not equal a tithe of the outgoing, would be a pretty expensive luxury. A ship or two a year would be ample for such a trade. The expense of importing under it would exceed five times that through New York, where the amount of consumption, and the abundance and perfection of the means employed, reduces the cost to the lowest point.

Numerous illustrations of this principle will occur to every merchant. Suppose a ship laden with silks and the more expensive textile fabrics, were to go to Charleston for a market. Her cargo would be sufficient to supply the State for years. In six months changes of style and fashion would render what might be unsold unmerchantable. How long would such a direct trade continue? It would never commence. Northern cities monopolize the importation of high priced goods, because their consumers are numerous enough to take whole cargoes while they are bright and fresh. Their customers exceed a hundred-fold the number that would ever find their way to any Southern city. Their merchants would always undersell the Southern importer on his own ground— would clean him out of the market in a month's time.

The proceeds of the Southern crops comes North simply *to pay Southern debts.* Take an illustration of this on a grand scale. Every year the value of merchandize going West over the Erie Canal, New York Central and Erie Railroads, exceeds that coming East over the same routes, by $100,000,000. This is a puzzle to many persons who do not reflect upon the course of trade in this country. They look upon the enormous excess of Western-bound freight as a proof of the extravagance or unsoundness of the West. It is simply the process by which that section gets pay for the products which it sells to the South. These debts Cotton pays. The Northern shipper takes it to Europe, brings back the proceeds, which are distributed by Northern merchants and factors to the creditors of the South, throughout the length and breadth of the - land. It is not convenient for the West to receive its pay through Norfolk, or Charleston, or Savannah, or New Orleans, but through *Northern cities,* and over interior routes of communication.

IF THE NORTH ARE THE CARRIERS FOR THE COUNTRY, THEY MUST CONTINUE TO PERFORM THE "EXCHANGES" FOR THE COUNTRY.

The preceding statement of the routine of business disposes of the great bugbear of *" the exchanges,"* amounting to fabulous millions, about which Wall street is in such tribulation, and which the South are going to snatch away from us, and with them all our wealth and greatness, leaving only ruins to mark the spot where New York once stood. Exchanges are simply links in a great chain which cannot be omitted till the whole is destroyed—results of business operations carried on between different sections of the country. The South, upon the sale of their Cotton, deliver their Northern factors, for collection, the bills drawn against the shipment. These bills are primarily used in adjusting the balances between England and the United States. Here is class of exchanges number *one*. As far as the South is concerned, the value, or proceeds of such bills are distributed among its Northern creditors, in which are embraced the Western farmer, as well as the Northern manufacturer and importer. Here is class of exchanges number *two*. The North will cease to perform these *exchanges* when the South cease to buy, or sell, or travel, or work plantations, or wear fine clothes—and not till then.

THE SOUTH CANNOT COMPETE WITH THE NORTH IN ANY OF THE INDUSTRIES REQUIRING SKILL.

Success in any pursuit is in exact ratio to the industry and skill used. The articles most perfectly finished, or best adapted to their objects will take the market, South as well as North, even if manufactured by Garrison. His mark could be easily scratched out. If he made the best article, Yancey, himself, if he stood in need of it would, for this purpose, lend the first hand. We won't libel him by allowing that he would prefer the poorer to the better article. It is skill, with its eyes open, that wins. At the North we do not blindfold our laborers, and then expect them to beat all mankind. The South have been constant in their attempts to establish manufactures, but unfortunately, as constantly unsuccessful, for the reason that no one, not even their own people, would buy their fabrics. These found the Yankee-made a better article, and deaf to all appeals to their Southern pride and patriotism, would have it. This is the secret of the failure of Southern manufactures. Southern people have no notion of reversing the universal law—the desire of possessing the best. We treat our manufacturers at the North the same way. If they cannot produce as good an article as Englishmen or Frenchmen, we patronize the foreigner without scruple. If the Southern manufacturer wishes to drive the Northern manufacturer out of his own neighborhood, he must excel him. If he can do so, to an extent equal to the cost of transportation, he will speedily shut our establishments, as we have his. They will have Northern made goods down South, even at the expense of every attempt at home manufacture.   Hear what William Gregg, Esq., one of the most intelligent gentlemen of South Carolina, and who has devoted his life, almost, to efforts to introduce manufactures into his State, says in a late number of *De Bow's Southern Review*, the great oracle of Secession and Southern commercial and manufacturing independence :

" The political sentiment of the South is decidedly and universally against the North, but the more powerful *pecuniary and commercial sentiment* has shown itself to be *with* the North, and opposed to the South, and if continued will lead to our ruin, both commercially and politically.   It is so thoroughly interwoven in the body politic that it may be seen in the every-day acts of our people, from the lowest grade of society to the highest.   If additional evidence is necessary to prove the positions above assumed, what better proof do we want than the fact that an humble, unpretending country or village merchant, who has not the means of going beyond Charleston to lay in his stock of merchandize, should consider it necessary to *obliterate every mark on a box, which would betray the fact that his stock of goods were purchased in Charleston, and not in New York*.   It has, for years past, been a common thing for country merchants to request that their packages *should be so marked as to leave no clue to their having been bought in Charleston*. Does not every one know that a wide-spread public sentiment has long existed all over the South which has caused a preference to be given to articles purchased at the North ?   It was quite a plume in the cap of a trader, to be able to say he was just from *New York*, and had purchased his supplies there.   So highly has that advantage been esteemed, by all classes of men, that the idea of enabling a merchant to go to New York to lay in his stock, would enlist the kindly friendship of rich endorsers, and if anything could induce a board of bank directors to make an extraordinary effort to *accommodate*, it would most surely be in the *good cause* of enabling a neighboring merchant to transfer his custom from Charleston to New York.

" The manufacture of shoes, saddlery and harness, hats, and ready-made clothing, are branches of industry that *ought not* to be driven out of any country by the general consumption of foreign-made articles in these branches of trade. So fashionable has it become to purchase everything from the *North*, and to *utterly* neglect home industry, that our young men scarcely ever think of employing a seamstress to make their shirts; indeed, so little patronage is, of late days, extended to that branch of industry, that there is not one young lady in twenty who is growing up with the expectation of making a good housewife, who knows how to make a shirt. These are articles that ought to be produced at home, but they have been permitted gradually to become a *fixed* article in the list of *imports* from the 'Yankees.' Indeed, we have so long been habitually supplied by the 'Yankees,' with the commonest necessity about a household, that we may be said to be *unprepared*, as a people, for *separate nationality*.

"Why should not every village at the South have its haberdasher to supply us with ready-made clothing, made by our own Southern women; a hatter to make our hats, and shoemakers to manufacture our ladies, gentlemens' and childrens shoes; also, establishments to make our wagons, carts, wheelbarrows and plows, our carriages and buggies? Why should our blacksmiths not make their own horseshoes, and horseshoe nails, now supplied to them by the 'Yankees?' Northern axes and hoe-handles should be banished the country, and every merchant that sells garden seeds should encourage the country people around to raise them, to be sold by the quantity to merchants, to be put up in packages and labeled, for sale by them. Large fortunes have been amassed at the *North* by the simple article of *garden seeds*, which can be so easily raised at the South. Many other articles, equally insignificant, and as easily dispensed with, compose an important link in the chain of out-goes for Yankee Notions, which, when put together, add a large sum to millions drawn from the South for articles that ought to be made at home.

"But, alas! how is the present course of things to be changed? Any attempt to set up one of the branches of business named, will be met with the difficulty that looms up against all Southern enterprise—*the want of home patronage*—which has led to the ruin of many promising establishments. Many machine shops, where engines were built, have been obliged, throughout the South, to give up for want of customers. The steamboat repairs, obliged to be done at the South, has assisted in sustaining manufactures of that branch of business in our Southern seaport cities, has secured success where, otherwise, failure would have been more common.

" The great shoe manufactory of Charleston failed for the
want of Southern patronage. The Charleston cotton factory
felt the same pressure, and was compelled to send Charleston-
made domestics to New York for sale, while thousands of
bales of Yankee domestics were being distributed throughout
the South to supply country merchants. The Saluda factory
started in 1834, with most brilliant prospects. That company
looked to Columbia for a market to absorb all their products.
It was soon found that in that early stage of manufacturing,
the Saluda company were under the necessity of sending their
goods to New York, while the South was almost wholly supplied by Northern manufactures. That company soon sunk
its capital, and went into new hands. The second company
labored under the same causes of embarassment, and sunk
another capital, and the concern went into the hands of a
third company, and is now managed by a fourth set of prop-
rietors. The DeKalb factory, near Camden, maintained a
sickly existence for many years from the same cause—want
of Southern patronage.

" The Augusta mills, on a large scale, commenced with
prospects as fair, and probably more encouraging than any at
the South, before they were fully under way, felt seriously
the embarassments of the want of a home-market, and had
to send their sound heavy sheetings, in large quantities, to
New York. That company finally sold out, and we believe
did not realize more than twenty cents on the dollar put in,
and if the interest be calculated as a part of the capital, the
principal was all lost.

" Many of the same parties started a large machine shop
in Augusta. That establishment also went down, and sunk
its entire capital from the same cause—the lack of Southern
patronage. The failure of the Augusta Cotton Mills has
done more to put back the progress of manufacturing at the
South than any failure that has taken place. With the Augusta company, some twenty-five or thirty manufacturing
establishments became embarassed, and others have dragged
out a sickly existence from the same cause—want of home
patronage."

The whole question is one of intelligence and skill. With
the present social organization South, any other result is impossible. Southern laborers are ignorant and unskilful. The
Negro is regarded as an inferior caste, with no function but
to labor. This becomes, consequently, a badge of degrada-

tion to all who are enforced to it. By necessary consequence it is avoided by all classes of whites. A people possessing such notions can never compete with those who hold labor as an honor, and united with intelligence and industry, as the surest path to respectability and wealth.

Another insurmountable obstacle to success in manufacturing in the Southern States, where negroes are employed, is the impossibility of introducing what may be termed the co-operative principle, by which each laborer is paid just in proportion to the value of his service—in other word, to the degree of skill and industry he exercises. The highest of all motives is thus constantly appealed to, and all employed unite their best efforts to a common end. Every person attending a particular step in the process is as eager for success as the owner of the establishment, as his own wages depend upon the amount and excellence of the work he turns out. Enforced labor can never be appealed to in this manner. It shirks everything it can. A factory in Lowell, worked by slaves, would necessarily break down beside one worked by freemen, to whom high wages were paid; for this reason, that the products of the former would be so bunglingly wrought that no one would buy them, while the amount produced would be so small as to give no return on the capital invested. The result in Lowell would be exactly the same as it has been in South Carolina.

THE PAST COMMERCIAL RELATIONS BETWEEN THE NORTH AND SOUTH MUST BE CONTINUED.

The difference between the two sections is not accidental, to be changed or cured by wishing, but is the inevitable result of premises, equally diverse in principle. While one remains the other must. Whatever the South have come North for, they must continue to come for, and will only be prevented by the existence of actual hostilities. As soon as these subside, the ordinary intercourse, founded on natural laws, must be resumed and continue.

From what, then, are the Southern people going to withdraw? Not from our trade and industries, unless they cease to consume; not from personal intercourse which necessarily follows trade; nor unless they determine to forego the luxuries of our *peculiar* civilization, which seems to have such charms for them. Never was more Southern money spent North, in traveling, and in places of recreation and amusement, than during the past year. These are not likely to lose their attractions. The opera is not going to leave New York for Atlanta or Montgomery; nor is Newport, nor Niagara, nor Saratoga, nor the White Mountains to be improvised in South Carolina or Mississippi. The South come North for these, by a law no stronger than for the luxuries and necessities of life. We hear a great deal said of what they are *going to do;* but results bragged of in advance never did come to pass, and never will, for the reason that true greatness and success is but the unfolding of the principle, or kind of life, that man, or society, or a people have within them. Let our merchants and manufacturers, who have so troubled themselves with apprehensions, trust to the laws that underlie human nature and human conduct, rather than noisy declamation and groundless assertions, and they will come out all right. If the South are not in humor to buy, and *pay* too, our goods can be kept on their shelves. A case of silks, or a bale of cottons, or a steam-engine, or a hogshead of bacon, had better be on hand than in bad debts.

The extent to which the relations between the two sections may be disturbed, and the degree of the consequent injury, must depend upon the Southern States. The Northern States have no other desire but to remain on terms of harmony. We have not yet made such fools of ourselves as to threaten, on account of political differences, to close our ports to any one ready to offer us a bargain, or purchase anything we produce. In case of a breach we must suffer, but we should neither starve nor go naked, as we fortunately produce among ourselves nine-tenths of the articles we consume. We should also get what we do not produce, *cotton*, and that, too,

in sufficient abundance. This great staple absorbs in its production almost the entire labor and capital of the South. Unfortunately for them, they can *neither eat nor drink it*—nor can
they *wear it*, unless they first send it North to be manufactured. The question of our procuring a supply depends
simply upon that of the existence of Southern society and
Southern institutions. These cannot exist without its production and sale ; and we will not do Southerners the injustice
to suppose, that in making their purchases, they will not
eagerly seek the parties who will supply the best article at
the cheapest rate, and these must always be found in the
Northern States.

RELATIVE DEGREE OF WEALTH AND MEANS OF PRO-
DUCTION NORTH AND SOUTH.

In the preceding pages we have shown that the commercial relations between the North and South are founded on
natural laws, and can only be interrupted by political disturbances. Nine-tenths of the imported articles that the South
consume are purchased at the North. The greater proportion of these can be obtained from no other quarter except at
a greatly increased cost. Secession, in itself, would exert no
considerable influence to change the course of trade between
the two sections, or diminish its amount. Of course prohibi-
tory, or retaliatory laws might, for a time, produce great disturbance, but in the end, the interests of both sections would
regulate their intercourse, as it does that between the United
States and Canada. The Southern trade, therefore, cannot
be lost, though great loss and suffering may be caused by its
temporary withdrawal. But in such an event the great bulk
of our present trade would remain to us, while the increase
of its volume in the Northern States, in one decade, growing
out of our increased population, would, as we shall show,
be fully equal to the entire trade we now enjoy with the
South. The population of the Free States advanced within

the last ten years from 13,434,781 to 18,951,814, or at the
rate of about 41 per cent. At a similar rate from 1860 to
1870, the annual gain will be about 780,000. Their means
of production and consumption increase much more rapidly
than numbers, from the new and improved agencies constantly
brought into their service.

All wealth is the product of labor and capital; but the
degree of its accumulation depends upon the skill with which
it is directed, the density of population, the variety of
industries practised, and the amount of capital invested.
Skill, or inventive genius, is the prime agent, as it creates
population by supplying the means of existence—food, clothing and shelter and a variety of pursuits, by teaching new
processes or methods. It realizes the fable of Cadmus. It
is the nucleus around which, as their vital principle, great ag-
gregations of men gather. An improvement in the manufacture of iron rendered possible the construction of railroads,
iron ships, and, in fact, all the great works of the day. Its
inventor proved to be more prolific, and has added a larger
number to the population of England and the United States
than .all the families of the country in which he was born.
Millions in England, to-day, owe their very existence to the
power-loom, the spinning-jenny, and the process of puddling
iron. Goodyear, by teaching how to combine India-rubber
with sulphur, has made himself the progenitor of thousands,
and, in time, of hundreds of thousands, even if he had not
left a lineal descendant. In the commerce of the country he
is, to-day, a larger figure than the State of Florida, as his
improvements send a larger amount of values into consumption. One of the finest towns of Massachusetts is an out-
growth of an improvement by Bigelow, in the manufacture
of *carpets*. By a process that enables one man, assisted by
machinery, to perform the labor of a hundred, he gives employment to ten times the number of those whose labor he
superseded, increases the population of his State by thousands, and the value of the property in it by millions. The
wealth of the age is in the inventive brain, which finds at the

South neither encouragement nor support. It is computed that the machinery at work in England, and driven by steam, performs the labor of 600,000,000 men. Hence the vast wealth of that country. The machinery running in Massachusetts has a power equal to 100,000,000 of men. Uneducated muscular energy is now a very poor commodity compared with the skill that makes servants of natural laws. This is the triumph of the age in which we live. From the creation almost to the present generation, man had been the sport of natural laws, or phenomena, regarding them with superstitious awe and terror. The forces that heaved the mountains were to him struggles of imprisoned offenders; while the agent that proclaims his thought as fast as his imagination can fly, was the voice of an enraged deity. But man at last doubled upon his pursuers. A greater than Rarey appeared, and fiercer subjects than Cruiser were tamed to more submissive attitudes. For a people to cut themselves off from the highest uses of such agencies is to accept a hopeless inferiority. The South accepts such, because they will not put themselves to the requisite training and education needed to direct their use. If we take the two extremes of this country, where the *peculiar institution* and mechanical skill have their highest emphasis—South Carolina and Massachusetts—we shall find that labor in the latter, assisted by skill, is four times as productive as that in the former, where it is performed by ignorant slaves. This is easily demonstrated by a comparison of the products and exports of the two States.

The value of articles produced in the Southern States, and going into commerce, can be easily ascertained; those of the extreme South consisting of Cotton, Sugar, Rice, Lumber and Naval Stores, of the shipments of which from the Southern ports, statements, carefully prepared, are annually published. The exports from the port of Charleston for the year 1859–60, both foreign and coastwise, according to the annual statement in the Charleston *Mercury*, and published in *De Bow's Southern Review* for October, 1860, were as follows:

Exports.	Bales.	Value.	Value.
COTTON.			
Foreign	386,770		
Coastwise	159,339		
Total	546,109	$24,574,905	
Deduct received from Georgia	75,000		
Total	471,109	3,575,000—$21,199,905	
RICE.	Tierces.		
Foreign	43,354		
Coastwise	94,219		
Total	137,573	3,439,325	
RICE—Rough.	Bushels.		
Foreign	91,273		
Coastwise	41,671		
Total	132,008	250,000	
LUMBER.	Feet.		
Foreign	5,447,478		
Coastwise	6,833,354		
Total	12,280,832	309,861	
	Bbls.		
Naval Stores	157,787	336,680	
Add 10 per cent. for other ports in the State		2,553,519	
Total for the State			$28,088,587

The South Carolina Railroad brings annually to Charleston about 200,000 bales of Cotton, received from the Georgia Railroads. But a portion grown in South Carolina, adjoining the Savannah River, goes to Savannah for shipment. The estimate we have made for the State is probably greater than the product. The total estimate for all articles is a liberal one—but to be beyond the possibility of error, we will estimate the total exports of the State for 1859–60, at $30,000,000. This aggregate is at the rate of $41 per head, of the whole population, estimating it at 725,000; or at the rate of $70 for each negro in the State, estimating the whole number to be 420,000.

Now, by way of comparison, let us see what is the amount and value of the products of the State of Massachusetts. The last census we have is that of 1855, a very full and complete one, taken by the State authorities. The total value of the articles produced that year was $295,820,681. Of the total aggregate, values to the amount $66,439,825 were products of agriculture and manufacture, the greater portion of which were consumed at *home*, leaving a balance of $229,380,856 of fabrics consumed in other States as generally as by the people in this. We give a list of some of these articles, with their values, as interesting and indubitable illustrations of the subject under discussion :

Articles.	Value.
Cotton goods....................................	$36,464,738
Woolen goods...................................	15,124,233
Iron and manufactures of iron...................	10,326,874
Steam engines and machinery....................	7,344,890
Paper...	4,643,680
Refined Sugars.................................	2,056,630
Sperm oil and candles.. :......................	6,813,290
Soap and Candles...............................	7,720,533
Boots and Shoes................................	37,489,923
Hats, caps and bonnets.........................	7,532,718
Sperm and whale oil and bone...................	7,766,996
Mackerel and cod...............................	2,829,640
Distilled liquors...............................	3,154,828
Clothing.......................................	9,061,896
Glass..	2,648,125
Musical instruments............................	2,291,680
Jewelry and watches............................	2,105,000
Cordage..	2,478,410
Mechanics' tools...............................	1,142,604
Manufactures of copper and brass...............	3,187,556
Cutlery..	1,200,279
Total.....................................	$173,384,523

The population of Massachusetts in 1855 was 1,137,000, or one twenty-fifth that of the United States. Now, instead of consuming only their share of those manufactures, which are consumed abroad and in other States as generally as at home, we will estimate that they consumed 15 per cent., or values to the amount of $34,407,128. Deducting this sum, there would be left $194,973,726 of manufactured articles, the products of the State entering into the commerce of the country in an equal degree as those of South Carolina. This aggregate would give an average production of $172 per head of articles contributed to the commerce of the country

—a sum more than four times greater than the average amount contributed per head by the population of South Carolina In the case of Massachusetts, articles exceeding $100,000,000 in value, the products of the State consumed on the spot, were deducted in the outset, which is at the rate of $100 per head.

In South Carolina the articles produced and consumed at home in the same way will not probably equal more than $25 per head, or say $20,000,000 in all. But we do not propose to go into this branch of the subject, but confine ourselves to the relative value of the products of the two States exported for general consumption.

Massachusetts, then, produces and sends into the channels of commerce of the country more than four times as much, per head, of her population as South Carolina. A mere description of the agencies employed in the two States will compel to such a conclusion, without the support of a voucher or a figure. Within the compass of 100 acres in the City of Lowell are agencies at work which, assisted by 15,000 laborers, more than one-half females, produce for general consumption fabrics exceeding in value more than one-half the whole exports of South Carolina. *Two* Lowells, consequently, are of greater moment than this State in commercial affairs. Philadelphia is a dozen South Carolinas rolled into one.

But this is not all. In the census of the products of the industry of Massachusetts, the profits of her investments in commerce, navigation, in banks, insurance companies and railroads, both at home and abroad, are not included. The value of such investments exceeds $200,000,000, a sum equaling the entire slave property of South Carolina, estimating it at $500 a head, and yielding an annual net profit very nearly equaling that of the entire slave labor of the State, taking out the cost of its maintenance.

The difference in amount of production between labor North and South, is no where better seen than in comparing that of the Southern field hands with that of operatives employed in the manufacture of cotton at the North. The value of cotton fabrics manufactured in Massachusetts, in 1855, equaled $37,104,000. The value of the raw material used (105,851,749 pounds,) being $10,585,174. The net profit added by capital and labor was $26,518,826. The number of operatives employed was 36,588, of which 23,000 were females. The average value of product per head was $725, or ten times greater than the average value of the products of labor in South Carolina. It may be said, to be sure, that part of the profit due to the manufacture of cotton belongs to capital. This is true. But were the cotton mills of Massachusetts transferred to South Carolina, they would remain idle for want of competent hands to run them. Capital locates itself in Massachusetts because it can be joined with industry and skill, which, combined, yield a reward exceeding ten-fold that of uneducated and unskilled labor. By virtue of her skill and industry, assisted by her capital, which is their product, *the State of Massachusetts sends annually into the commerce of the country, values greater than that of the entire cotton crop of the South!*

As a people produce so they consume. If Massachusetts manufactures and exports fabrics to the value of $194,973,726, she imports and consumes an equal amount. Her imports being seven times greater than South Carolina, her trade to the country is seven times as valuable. We have no doubt it is worth ten times as much. Other Northern communities equally rich, consume in the same proportion.

It is not our object to go into a lengthened argument upon any of the matters discussed, but to give illustrations that will apply to a whole class. In commerce and manufactures the South does not pretend to compete with the North. The Cotton States do not bring capital, inventive genius and intelligence to aid their industry. The wealth of the present day results from a combination of these. These States count half, or 2,500,000, of their population as *capital*. From 1850 to 1860, the North imported from Europe nearly 3,000,000 people. These, though freemen, are capital just as much as the Southern Slaves, as their yearly industries add a larger sum to the wealth of the country, though possessed by them-selves. To compare the North with the South, we should increase our numbers by the amount of our permanently in-vested productive capital. This would give us relatively twice or thrice our present numbers. The present population of the North is nearly double that of the South. Its productive capacity, as we have shown, is four times as great per head. When it is considered that for the support of the negro $20 or $25, on the average, is an ample allowance, including food and clothing, while at the North it must be five times as much per head, the conclusions stated cannot fail to be adopted by every person at all familiar with the subject.

The returns of the census of 1850 give very nearly the same results. Mr. Guthrie, in his Report on the finances for 1854-5, prepared a statement from this census of the total products in each State, with the average value for each per-son, and from which the following table is compiled:

STATES.	PRODUCTS PER HEAD.	STATES.	PRODUCTS PER HEAD.
Massachusetts	$166 60	Wisconsin	$68 41
Rhode Island	164 61	Mississippi	67 50
Connecticut	156 05	Iowa	65 47
California	149 60	Louisiana	65 00
New Jersey	120 62	Tennessee	63 10
New Hampshire	117 17	Georgia	61 45
New York	111 94	Virginia	59 42
Pennsylvania	99 30	South Carolina	56 91
Vermont	96 02	Utah	56 62
Illinois	89 04	Alabama	55 72
Missouri	83 06	Florida	54 77
Delaware	85 27	Arkansas	52 04
Maryland	83 65	District of Columbia	52 00
Ohio	75 62	Texas	51 13
Michigan	72 54	North Carolina	49 38
Kentucky	71 62	Minnesota	24 13
Maine	71 11	New Mexico	16 50
Indiana	69 12		

Such has been the progress in mechanical invention and in the manufacturing industries of the North, there is no doubt that the value of products, per head, in these, is four or five times greater than in the planting States. This excess is steadily increasing, and just to the degree that natural laws and agencies united with capital, are made to supercede muscular energy, especially that of ignorant and unskillful men.

The magnitude of the internal trade of Massachusetts is a striking illustration of the vastness of the products of her industry. The number of tons of merchandize carried on all the Railroads of the State, in 1859, was as follows:

ROADS.	TONS CARRIED.	ROADS.	TONS CARRIED.
Agricultural Branch	7,784	New Bedford and Taunton	47,147
Boston and Lowell	389,455	Newburyport	19,370
Boston and Maine	276,390	New London, W. and Palmer	34,000
Boston and Worcester	327,350	Norfolk County	29,171
Boston and Providence	259,938	Norwich and Worcester	117,445
Cape Cod Branch	42,285	Old Colony	199,298
Cheshire	125,477	Pittsfield and North Adams·	28,287
Connecticut River	102,442	Prov., Warren and Bristol	8,225
Eastern	114,593	Providence and Worcester	142,130
Easton Branch	9,940	South Shore	18,756
Essex	33,822	Stony Brook	17,906
Fairhaven Branch	10,165	Stoughton Branch	25,962
Fitchburg	413,923	Taunton Branch	50,126
Fitchburg and Worcester	30,718	Vermont and Mass	76,297
Lexington and West Cambridge	20,766	Western	448,345
Middleboro' and Taunton	13,172	Worcester and Nashua	101,426
Nashua and Lowell	174,973	Total	3,716,726

A part of the tonnage is duplicated, not more than 700,000 tons, however, leaving at least 3,000,000 as the actual tonnage for all the Roads. This amount for a single State North, is greater than the total tonnage of the Railroads of all the Southern States. At the low estimate of one hundred dollars per ton, the aggregate value would be $300,000,000, a sum considerably greater than the exports of all the Southern States, both Foreign and Coastwise. Such a comparison gives us a good idea of the superior productiveness of Northern industry over Southern. But this comparison by no means does justice to the North. A very large amount of the products of Massachusetts does not go upon the Railroads at all, but is shipped direct from the place of production—a large number of the manufacturing towns, such as Boston and vicinity, Fall River, Taunton, New Bedford, Newburyport, Salem and Lynn, lying upon tide-water.

THE MOUTHS OF THE MISSISSIPPI—WHERE ARE THEY?

A few years ago the only method of getting the produce of the greater portion of the Western States to market was to float it by its own gravity down the Mississippi. To give us the free use of this river and its outlet, and to avoid a constant source of bickering and quarrel with a foreign power, the territory of Louisiana was purchased. But this did not accomplish all that was needed. The consumers of this produce lay to the north-east, rendering necessary a circuit of some four thousand miles to reach districts separated only by as many hundred. The people of New York, consequently, set to work to open another outlet for the great valley—in effect to turn its great river into their own magnificent harbor. With this view the Erie Canal was constructed; a work of small capacity in the outset, but still sufficient to accomplish vast results, instantly reducing the cost of transporting a ton of merchandize from Buffalo to New York from $100 to $15.

Such a result, and the great commercial advantages that followed, led the Eastern States of Pennsylvania, Maryland and Virginia, and all the States bordering the Lakes, to undertake similar works. The State of Pennsylvania constructed a canal from the Susquehanna to the Ohio River, and extensions from this river to Lake Erie, and to the line of Ohio. This State constructed two canals extending from its southern to its northern boundary. Indiana undertook a similar work, extending from the north-east to the south-west corner of the State. Illinois commenced a canal to unite Lake Michigan with her great river, which was completed in 1848. These works which, at the time they were commenced, were regarded as superior to all other modes of transportation of property, as well as persons, led to a great change in the direction of Western produce. Instead of being sent, every pound of it, down the Mississippi as formerly, increasing quantities were yearly turned into the new routes.

But Canals could be constructed only in a few localities. A new and more efficient agency, the greatest achievement of modern times, the *Railroad*, came into play. Practicable everywhere, they were commenced in every part of the country, and in the decade just closed, more than 10,000 miles, have been constructed in the North-Western States alone Nearly every mile was designed to be, and is, tributary to the works of the North-Eastern States, including Pennsylvania and Maryland, and is but carrying out the objects which gave birth to the Erie Canal. From Lake Michigan eleven great lines of railroad radiate, striking the Mississippi and Ohio at as many points, the extremes being Lacrosse and Cincinnati. Four great lines run directly East from the Mississippi, forming connections with others leading to the seaboard. Nine great railroads have been constructed between the Ohio and Lake Erie. The routes described are trunks for a net of less important lines, covering the whole West, and supply the means for sending North and East the whole of its products. In the meantime the capacity of the Erie Canal has been increased five-fold. Five great lines of railroad have also been constructed, extending from the Atlantic to Lake Erie and the Ohio River, and affording abundant means for transporting, at a cheap rate, the entire production of the interior. The cost of the works, constructed to change the direction of the commerce of the Mississippi, cannot be less than $500,000,000, or about one-half the cost of all the railroads and canals of the United States !

The results accomplished have been as vast as the means employed. Forty-nine fiftieths of all the produce of the Free States of the West are turned over the new channels leading directly to the districts of consumption. The importance of the Mississippi river and its outlets, as channels of commerce, consequently, has been reduced in an equal degree. If the freedom of its navigation should be threatened, we have the satisfaction of knowing that we have already secured to ourselves, through new channels under our own control, the trade of the greater and better portions of the valley watered by this river. This trade, already of vast magnitude and value, is yearly swelling in volume. Every day are we enlarging the area tributary to the East. Nearly all the breadstuffs, and the greater part of the animal food raised in the West, comes directly to us. Cotton begins to follow in the same direction. Nothing but the inability of our railroads for want of rolling stock, prevented very large quantities from coming North the present year over the interior routes. The threatened disturbances on the Southern frontier will have an immediate effect to increase the quantity. As soon as the necessary facilities are supplied there is no doubt that cotton will come forward in large quantities, both for manufacture and exportation. In fact, the trade of every foot of the valley of the Mississippi is a subject of legitimate competition by our merchants, and may conveniently be brought into our harbors over our own works. The navigable waters of the Ohio come within about three hundred miles of those of the Atlantic, while those of the great Lakes are within one hundred and eighty. Freight can as well go up as down the river, while the loss from insurance and delay of transportation by the mouth of the river and around the Florida Keys, will render the interior the cheaper route, to say nothing of its greater convenience, and the low rates between the Eastern Atlantic cities and Europe.

In order to give a clear idea of the amount of Western produce sent *East* over artificial lines of improvement, we annex a table of the *through* Eastern bound freight of the five great routes—the Erie Canal, New York Central, New York and Erie, Pennsylvania, and Baltimore and Ohio Railroads, since 1836, in which year the Western trade over the Erie Canal may be said to have commenced. The tolls on the New York Central Railroad were removed in 1851, the Erie Railroad was opened in the same year. The Pennsylvania Railroad was opened in 1852, so as to commence a through business in connection with the Public Works of Pennsylvania. The Baltimore and Ohio Railroad was also opened in 1852. The tons given are those received at the Western terminus of each work, and delivered at tide-water:

Year.	Tons Western produce coming to tide by Erie Canal	Do. do. by New York Central Railroad.	Do. do. by New York and Erie Railroad.	Do. do. by Penn'a Railroad.	Do. do. by Balt. and Ohio Railrond.	Total tons to tide-water from West. States.
1836	54,219	....	....	....	....	54,219
1837	56,255	....	....	....	....	55,255
1838	83,233	....	....	....	....	83,233
1839	121,671	....	....	....	....	121,671
1840	158,148	....	....	....	....	159,148
1841	224,176	....	....	....	....	224,176
1842	221,477	....	....	....	....	221,477
1843	256,376	....	....	....	....	256,376
1844	306,025	....	....	....	....	308,025
1845	304,551	....	....	....	....	304,551
1846	506,830	....	....	....	....	506,830
1847	812,840	....	....	....	....	812,940
1848	650,154	....	....	...	....	650,154
1849	768,659	....	....	....	....	768,659
1850	773,859	....	....	....	....	773,859
1851	966,993	....	....	....	....	966,993
1852	1,151,978	48,000	48,000	....	....	1,247,978
1853	1,213,690	70,000	70,000	38,837	21,014	1,413,641
1854	1,100,526	117,000	77,161	53,825	90,368	1,438,880
1855	1,092,876	147,500	113,331	106,407	72,779	1,532,893
1856	1,212,550	172,781	202,682	88,707	145,598	1,822,323
1857	919,998	179,647	157,820	94,905	126,323	1,478,693
1858	1,273,099	229,275	224,886	141,268	171,084	2,039,611
1859	1,036,634	234,241	171,206	129,767	135,127	1,706,775
1860	1,500,000	293,520	300,000	150,000	149,651	2,393,171
Total	16,763,816	1,495,923	1,357,086	803,716	912,544	21,348,085

The number of tons of Western Produce delivered annually at tide water over these routes, exceed twice the number of tons of all kinds of produce delivered at New Orleans, and considerably exceed the same in value. The freight over the New York routes is so classified that an accurate idea can be formed of its value. The subjoined statement will show the tonnage of the two great railroads of the State for 1860, with the estimate value of each class of freight:

ARTICLES.	TRANSPORTED BY CENTRAL RAILROAD.		TRANSPORTED BY ERIE RAILROAD.	
	Tons.	Value.	Tons.	Value.
Products of forest	42,705	$846,100	118,899	$2,377,780
Products of animals	223,362	44,672,400	201,823	40,364,600
Vegetable food	343,872	13,754,880	197,232	7,889,280
Other agricultural products	39,167	587,520	19,909	298,635
Manufactures	77,256	19,314,000	113,948	27,487,000
Merchandise	201,587	100,793,500	198,610	99,305,000
Miscellaneous	100,632	1,006,320	269,140	2,591,400
Total	1,028,381	$180,974,720	1,119,551	$180,613,695

In the above statement products of the forest are valued at $20 the ton; products of animals at $200; vegetable food at $50; other agricultural products at $15; manufactures at $250; merchandize at $500, and miscellaneous freight at $10 per ton. The total tonnage of both roads was 2,167,736, valued at $361,893,425. The number of tons carried on the New York Canals for 1859 was 3,781,684, valued at $132,-560,758. We have received only a statement of freight coming to tide-water for 1860, which equaled 2,916,066 tons, valued at $80,458,585, against 2,121,672 tons for 1859, valued at $53,175,312. Assuming a rate of increase equal to that coming to tide-water, of freight moving in other directions, the total tonnage on the Canal the past year was 5,216,464 tons, equaling in value $182,932,800. The total tonnage of the three routes was 7,384,210, valued at $544,186,705. The tonnage of the Pennsylvania Railroad the past year, exclusive of coal, was 823,302 tons; that of the Baltimore and Ohio Railroad 592,559. The total tonnage of the five great outlets of the Lakes and Mississippi Valley, eastward, exclusive of the Ogdenburg and Grand Trunk Railroads and Canadian Canals was 8,799,961 tons, equaling in value very nearly, if not quite, $700,000,000!

This vast commerce, nearly every dollar of which is due to the construction of our Public Works, is one of the most marvelous creations of modern times. It strikingly illustrates the method of our people on this Continent, and how insufficient are natural advantages unless backed by energy and skill, against those who possess hardly anything but these qualities.

Thirty-six years ago it cost $100 the ton to transport a ton of merchandize over either of the three routes between New York and Lake Erie. Over the Erie Canal the cost per ton the past year, between the same points, averaged only $3. The effect of such reduction, in transportation charges, was to enlarge in an equal degree the area of the trade of this great work. With a cost of $10 per ton this area would be described by a line drawn only a few miles from the shores of the Great Lakes. Every cent below this rate pushed this boundary in every direction further inland. The reduction of a dollar in transportation charges between Buffalo and New York has the effect to increase the radius of this boundary fifty miles. Assuming the previous length of such radius to have been two hundred miles, the extent of territories made tributary to the Canal, and to the trade of the City, would equal 35,000 square miles. The reduction of another dollar per ton on cost of transportation would annex another area equal to 45,000 square miles.

This has been the method of the aggressions of the people of the manufacturing and commercial States of the East upon the interior. By constant reductions in the cost of transportation they have steadily pushed further and further inland the line of debatable ground between the artificial and natural outlets of the great valley, till they have turned directly to themselves almost the entire trade of the North-West.

No statement can convey an adequate idea of the extent of the trade in breadstuffs of the City of New York. The deliveries from the Canal at tide-water, the past year, equaled 1,367,563 tons, valued at $48,183,044. The Erie and Central Railroads transported (nearly all to tide-water) 540,000 tons of vegetable food. Estimating 500,000 tons of this amount to be breadstuffs, mostly Flour, and worth $50 per ton, its value was equal to $25,000,000. The aggregate tonnage brought to tide-water by the three routes was worth at least $73,184,044. Reducing the barrels of Flour to bushels, the whole number of bushels that came to the New York market the past year, through her three channels, equaled 71,384,143 bushels!

Of animal food the two railroads brought to tide-water the past year, 425,185 tons, worth on the average $200 per ton, and in the aggregate $85,037,000. The Canal brought 12,574 tons, valued at $2,766,694. The aggregate value brought by the three routes was $87,803,694. The aggregate tonnage of breadstuffs and animal food brought to tide-water, the past year, was 2,305,321 tons, and their aggregate value $160,-

906,778, a sum nearly, if not quite, equal to the value of the Cotton crop of the United States the past year. If we add the value of the vegetable and animal food brought to tide-water, the past year, from the Western States over the Pennsylvania and Baltimore and Ohio Railroads, the aggregate will be over $200,000,000!

Against this movement on the Eastern routes, there were received at New Orleans, the past year, by way of the Mississippi River, 965,860 barrels of Flour, 13,116 sacks of Wheat, 1,722,037 sacks of Corn, 659,550 bushels of Oats, 216,523 barrels and 1,874 hogsheads of Pork, 83,922 barrels of Lard, 44,934 barrels and tierces of Beef, and 82,819 casks and hogsheads of Bacon. Reducing the Flour to bushels, the total number of bushels of grain received at New Orleans was 5,687,399, against 71,384,143 received at tide-water over the New York lines, or at least 85,000,000 bushels over all the five great Eastern outlets. The tons of animal food received at New Orleans the past year, was 95,700, against 437,759 by the New York routes, or adding the tonnage of animal food brought by the Pennsylvania and Baltimore and Ohio Railroads, against, probably, 525,000 tons on the five Eastern outlets of the great valley.

The *exports* of the above articles from New Orleans, the past year, both foreign and coastwise, were as follows :

EXPORTS TO	FLOUR.	PORK.	BACON.	LARD.	BEEF.	CORN.
	Bbls.	Bbls.	Casks.	Bbls.	Bbls.	Sacks.
New York	10,862	868	271	9,948	9,878	37,243
Boston	41,524	2,097	91	1,061	1,699	22,410
Philadelphia	....	....	....	260	10	....
Baltimore	....	....	....	....	....	....
Other Coastwise Ports	247,231	45,572	28,565	7,396	3,019	498,916
Great Britain	6,341	89	....	7,846	5,495	52,448
Cuba	6,478	1,307	1,461	37,380	735	27,065
Other Foreign Ports	74,115	3,120	305	6,461	863	14,288
Total	386,511	53,050	30,693	70,852	21,699	652,370

Of the breadstuffs exported from New Orleans the past year, only 58,727 barrels of Flour and 112,101 sacks of Corn

were sent to the Eastern States and Great Britain, the value
of which did not exceed $576,564. Of Provisions there were
exported in the same direction 3,055 barrels of Pork, 362
casks of Bacon, 18,871 barrels of Lard, and 17,082 barrels
of Beef, the value of the whole not exceeding $600,000. In
other words, the total exports of breadstuffs and provisions,
the products of the Mississippi Valley, sent to the Eastern
States and Great Britain, the past year, did not exceed
$1,200,000 in value. The exports coastwise were to Gulf ports;
and to other Foreign ports—Mexico and the West Indies.
These exports would have gone by way of the Mississippi
for convenience of distribution, whoever held the mouth of
that River. The imports into New Orleans, for consumption,
are not to be affected by political changes unless they weaken
its ability to consume.

These facts show how small a proportion of the products
of the North-Western States goes to market by way of the
Mississippi River. The produce received at New Orleans
came almost entirely from the Southern States—the Flour
from St. Louis, and the Corn and Bacon from Kentucky and
Tennessee. It is not probable that one-fiftieth of the total
exports of grain from the North-West went down the Mississippi. Of other articles of export, Wool, Lumber, Butter,
Cheese, Hides, etc., etc., no portion whatever is sent down the
Mississippi—the whole going direct to the Eastern States.

These facts are stated, not by way of invidious comparison,
but to show the power that resides in the North and East by
virtue of their numbers, wealth, industries and means of intercommunication, and how completely these sections have
changed the direction of the great routes of commerce of the
interior. The free navigation of the Mississippi, which only
a few years ago was considered so indispensable, is for the
North-Western States an imaginary rather than a real necessity. They would not, of course, consent that any of their
outlets should be closed, as it might increase the exactions of
others, and, as extraordinary emergencies might occur, creat-
ing interruptions in those now used. It is not probable that

the people of New Orleans ever will allow the free navigation of its great feeder to be interfered with, as this would threaten the destruction of their wealth and trade. The peaceable effect of Secession may be to close its mouth, in which event the entire trade of the Valley could be easily, and in the end to the convenience and benefit of all, sent over the Northern and Eastern routes.

It may be assumed that the cotton grown in Tennessee, a portion of Alabama, all Mississippi and Arkansas, and a part of Louisiana, can be delivered at Cairo as cheaply as at New Orleans. From Cairo to New York, $4 a bale, or $16 a ton, would afford a fair business to the carrier. From New Orleans to New York, by the outside route, including charges at the former place, and insurance, the rate cannot be estimated at less than a cent to a cent and a quarter per pound. In favor of the interior route is time, climate and uniform health. There is now annually consumed in the Northern and Eastern States, nearly one million of bales. Our manufacturing establishments are already receiving large amounts through the interior routes, which will be steadily increased till the greater part consumed reaches them in this manner. All the railroads connecting the interior with the Eastern States, are making extensive provision for this new traffic, which is certain to be secured by our method of low charges, and by the great advantages which New York, Boston and Philadelphia present as the ports of shipment.

If, as now appears certain, New Orleans follows in the wake of Charleston, that port will be speedily closed. Secession by a State is followed by precisely the same steps as the commission of a wrong by an individual. He arms himself, and immediately commences erecting barriers for defence. Charleston has filled the channel of her harbor with sunken ships, a defence for an anticipated attack, and destroyed her commerce at the same time. New Orleans will necessarily repeat the example set her, and virtually close her port. With Secession, the day of her commercial greatness is past. Hereafter, the trade peculiar to her must flow North. From

the present year, shall we number *Cotton* received through
our interior routes as an important item in our exports. Once
gained, it is a business we shall never lose. With it we shall
sweep the trade of the whole interior. Already are the railroads of the Western States and the connecting lines to the
Eastern, glutted with freights which, up to the present year,
went down the Mississippi to New Orleans. There is no
doubt that the trade, both foreign and domestic, of the great
Eastern cities, the present year, will exceed in amount that
of any one in their past history. They will retain all they
had, while Secession will hand over to them the greater part
of that which in times of peace had concentrated itself in the
cities of the Gulf and the Lower Mississippi.

While, with the Public Works now constructed, the Northern cities have already monopolized the greater portion of the
trade of the interior, their means for extending this trade are
yearly increasing. The Erie Canal opens this year, for the
first time, with an available depth of water of seven feet.
The great lines of Railroads are steadily increasing their facilities and accommodations. Rates are so graduated to
command freight. The manner in which these have been
steadily reduced on the Erie Canal, so as to secure trade and
meet the competition of other routes, is strikingly illustrated
by the following table, which shows the cost of transportation over this work, including tolls, since 1836 :

YEAR.	FROM ALBANY TO BUFFALO.	FROM BUFFALO TO ALBANY.	YEAR.	FROM ALBANY TO BUFFALO.	FROM BUFFALO TO ALBANY.
	Cost per ton.	Cost per ton.		Cost per ton.	Cost per ton.
1836···	$21.00	$7.13	1848···	$7.80	$5.37
1837···	18 60	7.50	1849···	7.80	5.18
1838···	17.80	6 76	1850···	7.20	5 49
1839···	17.80	6.44	1851···	6 20	4.71
1840···	16.60	7.50	1852···	5.20	4.90
1841···	12.20	6 57	1853···	5.60	5 18
1842···	13.20	6 02	1854···	5.00	4.81
1843···	11.20	5.56	1855···	5.00	4.81
1844···	13.00	5.56	1856···	5.40	5.56
1845···	9.60	6.57	1857···	4.80	4.26
1846···	8.00	5 92	1858···	2.80	3 14
1847···	7.80	7.13	1859···	2.40	2.87

The rates of charges on the Railroads have been reduced in an equal degree. In 1856, the Central and Erie Railroads received *three* cents for every ton of freight moved one mile. In 1860 they received only *two* cents for the same service. The economies introduced into the management of these roads have probably reduced the expenses to an equal extent.

" Secession" is likely to lead to the construction of another work of great importance in connection with the trade of the West, and which has long occupied public attention—a ship canal between Lake Michigan, at Chicago, and the Illinois River. It is well known that the summit between the Lake and the River is only eight feet. A comparatively small sum only, considering the result to be achieved, is required for this work, which would send a portion of the waters of the three great upper Lakes down the Mississippi! The flow of this water would render the Illinois River navigable at all times, and as far as its commerce and that of its great recipient are concerned, their mouths would be literally on Lake Michigan. The realization of this project cannot be far off, when the works necessary to give a Northerly direction to all portions of the great valley will be complete.

WHERE SHALL THE BORDER STATES GO?

In the Cotton States the influence of climate has, in their opinion, rendered African Slavery a necessity, an institution to be cherished and maintained. The people there see nothing better in the future than what this is to bring. It being their capital, upon the earnings of which they depend for existence, its protection and development engross their whole being. Hence the striking contrasts they present in sentiment, opinion and aims to the people of the Free States. The two are antipodes. But these diversities come into direct collision in the *Border States*, where slavery exists by accident, and must in time certainly disappear, yielding to industries better adapted to their climate and resources. In a crisis like the

present, it is natural that there should be great sympathy between the people of these States and those further South, as
both are still supporting an institution the morality of which,
they fancy, is attacked, casting upon both the same implica-
tion, and which both of them so strenuously resent. On the
other hand it is felt that from the influences at work, and
which they cannot resist, the Border States must become more
and more like the Free States, towards which they now feel a
strong antipathy, and less like their Southern brethren, with
whom they are in close sympathy. Under such circumstances
the question of the direction in which they shall go is one of
the utmost importance as well as of embarrassment.

It is, without doubt, for their interest to have their present
political *status* continue, unless they accept the extreme pro-
position that the measure best calculated to promote their interest is that which soonest puts an end to slavery, as the
division of the country upon their northern frontier would be
sure to do. But extreme measures are always to be avoided,
and it is of the highest importance that one kind of labor
should, as fast as it disappears, be replaced by another. It is
for the interest of the Border States, therefore, to have the
Union continue as it is, so that while the slave is gradually
moved toward the Cotton States, his place shall be supplied
by an influx of free labor from the North.

Experience has fully proved that in the Border States there
is no more room for slaves. Take for illustration the case of
Virginia. The number of slaves in this State has increased,
from 1830 to 1860, from 469,009 to 495,000, or at the
rate of only about five per cent. for the thirty years. The
free population in the meantime had increased from 694,000
to 1,097,000, or at the rate of forty-three per cent. Slave
labor in this State by no means increases in ratio to the
amount of new land brought into cultivation. The moment
this is fully occupied the number will immediately begin to
decrease. Virginia, therefore, has no more room for slaves.
If the slave trade should be opened it would not add one to
her present number, except so far as it would check the ex-

portation to other States. This is the very thing that Virginia
has most to fear. The opening of this trade would strike a
fatal blow at the value of property which she considers worth
at least $300,000,000, and the yearly exportation of which
produces many millions. To retain the number of slaves
annually exported, would overstock her own market, and
largely reduce the aggregate value of slaves in the State, notwithstanding their greatly increased numbers. Virginia considers it indispensable to retain the monopoly of supplying
the new States with negroes. The cry on the other hand,
from those States is *cheap labor*, which they fancy they can get
only by opening the slave trade.

If, therefore, it be the interest of Virginia to maintain
slavery, this is only possible *in* the Union. Out of it, the.
price of slaves would fall to a degree that would render the
whole institution an incumbrance not worth maintaining. In
case of dissolution, the fear of losing them would send them
all out of the State in a comparatively short time. Should
Virginia join the Southern Confederacy, a conflict of interest
would leave her without position or influence, even while she
retained her slaves, and an object of aversion and distrust, as
she would soon lose them to a degree to show she must even-
tually become a Free State. The alternative, consequently,
presented is, whether she shall change her position as the most
central and influential State in the present Confederacy, or
become an unwelcome and suspected member of one to which
all her interests are hostile, and which must be without strength
dignity or power.

But while Virginia has no more room for slaves, she has
still boundless room for *freemen*. As man is the most valuable
product of society, the excellence of its institutions and industries are to be measured in exact ratio of their tendency
to promote increase of numbers, assuming, of course, a corresponding increase in the means for their support. This is a
standard universally acknowledged, and by none more em-
phatically than Virginia. As a means of increasing her
population and wealth, she has incurred a debt of nearly

$40,000,000, which she proposes greatly to increase before
the completion of her system. By means of these works she
hopes to develope the boundless wealth that lies hid in her
soil, to turn to use her vast water power, and to build up depots of trade upon her magnificent harbors. This she can
only do by the use of a higher grade labor than she now em-
ploys. A population devoted to agriculture, after reaching a
certain point, always remains stationary. It reached that
point in Eastern Virginia forty years ago. In this period the
whole population of the country increased 350 per cent.
Could Virginia have retained her natural increase she would
now have had a population of 3,628,826, or nearly as great
as that of New York, instead of 1,593,000, the present number. Pennsylvania, an adjoining State, with no greater advantages, and greatly inferior in resources in many respects,
had a less population in 1820 than Virginia. It has one now
nearly twice as great, with ten-fold greater wealth.

The cause of the difference between the two is just as pal-
pable as the difference itself. Pennsylvania cultivates a
variety of pursuits; consequently she has a population of 64
to the square mile, against 26 in Virginia. Massachusetts,
with her sterile soil and inhospitable climate, has a population
of 160 to the square mile. The same ratio would give Virginia a population of 10,000,000! If the resources of
Virginia were as thoroughly cultivated as those of Massachusetts, she would have to-day a population of 20,000,000!
She has the means of giving lucrative employment and an
ample support to such a population. The creation of it upon
her own soil, and within a comparatively short time, rests
solely upon the question of the industries she may adopt.
The agricultural population of Massachusetts to-day is not as
large as it was fifty years ago, yet her total population in the
meantime has gone from 474,000 to 1,231,000, and very nearly
in ratio with the increase for the whole country. She has
been true to the spirit and genius of the age, and has, consequently, kept up with its progress. Virginia, on the other
hand, has hardly begun to appropriate to herself the agencies

and powers upon which progress in wealth and population
in these modern times is based. Since 1810, the ratio of increase of her numbers has been only about one half as great
as that of England and Wales. The increase of the population of the former, from 1810 to 1850, was from 974,622 to
1,421,662, or at the rate of 45 per cent. That of England
and Wales, from 1811 to 1851, went from 11,970,120 to 20,-
816,351, or at the rate of 80 per cent. This is a fact which
must strike most people with astonishment. Yet there is no
doubt that with the use of the same means that have increased so rapidly the population of England, every emigrant
sent out by Virginia to the new States might have been more
profitably employed at home. She has room for ten times
her present population, without being crowded. There is no
State in the Union which should have so large a population;
none in which labor should be more productive or better
paid.

In which direction, then, in the present crisis, shall Virginia
incline? To a system which, with vast resources, has rendered her progress in population, for the past forty years, only
about one-half as great as that of England, and which must
soon bring even this slow increase to a dead stand? or to
one that duplicates the population of the whole country every
twenty-five years, and increases its power, and wealth, and
means of support, in much greater ratio? Will she join a
Confederacy of which she must constitute the mere append-
age to a central power far removed and hostile to all her interests, or will she remain as the influential member of the
one that has given her all her power, dignity and historical
influence, which protects whatever she conceives to be her
interest, and under the fostering care of which she can unfold in just such directions as may suit the tastes, habits and
industries of her people?

Whatever direction the Border States may take they must
daily more and more resemble the Free States, both in their
industries and ideas. They have a similarity of climate and
soil, and which pre-eminently invite the introduction and use

of the mechanic arts, and a high grade of agricultural labor. With homogeneousness of interest there will also of ideas. This really would be most rapidly promoted by going with the South, as dissolution would put an end to slavery, when the last difference between the Border and Free States would be removed, and their reunion would take place as a matter of course. But even should they assume to go South, such would be the disastrous results, that reconstruction would follow as a matter of necessity, but not until a sacrifice of material interests had been made which would take a gene- ration to repair.

The Southern States secede, to escape what they term the Anti-Slavery tendencies of the North. But they carry with them precisely the same tendencies, and from which escape is impossible. The contrasts in the physical features and ma- terial conditions of portions of most of the Slave States are as striking as between these and the Free States, and, in many cases, more so. Take Virginia. Here is a standing quarrel, as bitter and well defined as those between Massachusetts and South Carolina. It is the same story. In the Eastern portion the slave predominates ; in the Western, freemen. The slaveholding counties have now the advantage in the Legislature. This gives them control in all matters of taxa- tion, and in a thousand questions of local legislation. The Western portion increases rapidly ; the Eastern not at all. The West is healthy, full of minerals, and well adapted to manufactures. The East is wanting in all these. The West is too near the Ohio to trust the negro in it. Ilis place is being taken by white laborers. Here is the irrepressible con- flict raging on *Southern* soil. The West complains that the slave is represented in the legislature without bearing his proportion of tax. The two sections are becoming more and more antagonistic. Their differences are stated with as much acrimony as those between the North and South. How is this element of disunion to be quelled ? Virginia can escape from it no more in a Southern Confederacy than in the Union. It will continue till one party or the other goes to the wall

It is not difficult to see on which side victory inclines. In 1864 the question of representation is to be submitted to the popular vote, when the West will have matters her own way. How is such a rebellion to be put down in the new Confederacy? It will not be confined to Virginia, nor to North Carolina, nor to Tennessee. The whole range of the Alleghanies to within one hundred and fifty miles of the Gulf, is full of *treasonable* elements—iron, coal, lead, copper and zinc—with a fertile soil, and a climate admirably adapted to white labor and the mechanic arts. It will soon be the theatre of industries in which the unlettered slave can never take part. Along this great highway has the column of Northmen already commenced its grand march, which the South can never for a moment stay, unless they disembowel the earth of its treasures, taint the pure air, and smite with sterility the soil.

In its progress Northern society does not ask or desire quiet. All progress is disturbance—displacement, in which the ghost of the old is not yielded without a struggle. If the South desire quiet, they must not include one foot of Territory about which it can be debated whether it be better adapted to Slavery or Freedom. If they do, then the only course will be to obliterate State lines altogether, and establish the despotism of perpetual silence. This is the only escape from the discussion of vexed questions. To such a result if it be successful, Secession must come. If the old lines are preserved, the new Ship of State will be manned by a mutinous crew, who will in time use and capture it, or compel a division of both vessel and cargo. Would it not be well for the South to consider these things before the fatal step be taken and ask whether it be not better

" To bear the ills that are,
Than fly to others that they know not of ? "

EFFECT OF SECESSION ON THE MATERIAL INTERESTS
OF THE SOUTH.

The South produce two or three staples which they can neither consume nor convert into forms fitting them for use.

Their labor is of the lowest grade and, consequently, only available within a very limited range. As the individual with only one faculty is at the mercy of every accident, so is a nation with only one kind of industry. When this fails, or is interrupted, its existence is threatened. It must employ foreigners, who may become enemies, to perform its most important functions. The South produce cotton, but having neither ships nor sailors, have to employ the North to take it to market, and bring back the proceeds. If the North are enemies, then an enemy must be employed. The South depend upon the North for the materials that give military power; the means of working their plantations, and moving their products. In fact, nearly the entire commercial machinery of the South is moved by the North. The South is poor for money, the North rich. United as one nation, the strength and means of one section become that of the other. Previous to the Secession movement, the Southern States were getting from the Northern States and from Europe, the means for their railroads as fast as they could show any claims to credit. Capital, though a most sensitive thing, is cosmopolitan. That of the world stands ready for the service of the person who bids highest, other things being equal. United with industry and skill, it carries man forward in his grand march. It is the *sine qua non* of progress. Thrown upon their own accumulations, a community would be a generation in accomplishing results, for which two or three years would be ample, using the capital of others. In the Western States, 10,000 miles of railroad have been constructed within ten years, which have cost $400,000,000, nearly the whole amount of which was supplied from the accumulations of the East and Europe. The profits of this investment in the increased value given to other kinds of property, and in causing other investments in lands, buildings, manufactures and commerce, have been three or four hundred per cent. greater than the cost of the railroads. In other words, the Western States, simply by the use of other people's money, have put into their pockets three or four times the amount. In addition, the loans are perpetual, at a low rate of interest, and will work for all time in adding to the marvelous results already accomplished.

Now, if the Western States had been in relations of alienation or hostility to the Eastern, they would have hardly had the first mile of railroad, or a canal—not one-half their present population, nor one-tenth their wealth. All this is too plain to require demonstration. Their roads have been constructed, and the Southern States, which were about ten years behind, were taking their place. But instead of maintaining the relations that accomplished such wonders for the West, they are placing themselves in hostile attitudes to all mankind, which will cut them off from every particle of capital not their own, bring all their improvements to a full stop, paralyze all their industries, and leave them in a condition of the most pitiable exhaustion and prostration. Take the case of Texas, the people of which are now so rampant for Secession. Of all Southern States she is most in need of capital, particularly to construct her public works. In her immense area she has no navigable rivers, and is absolutely without the means of sending her produce to market. Twenty-five million of dollars spent in railroads in this State would add ten times this sum to the wealth of her people. With Secession, not a dollar of this $25,000,000 can be had. She recently sent Mr. V. K. Stevenson, a gentleman well known in railroad circles, to Europe, to negotiate for the means to construct her proposed Railroad to the Pacific. He brought with him a *carte blanche* for a contract for the construction of the road, which would have been worth a hundred million to the State, but Secession has completely defeated the whole project. Her other roads in progress will now come to a full stand. Yet her people are rushing as madly towards Secession as if it were some grand carnival. They apparently have not the slightest idea that all this is to produce any change in their relations to *capital*. They think they can destroy, in a fit of mad sport, the fair fabric of Government, and find it still shielding and protecting them when they recover from their present delerium.

When the results of Secession are seen, and they must speedily follow, there must be an intense reaction. The people of Texas have really no hostility to the Union, but have caught the wild impulse of Secession, and while they are under its influence, they think it a fine thing to destroy our Government, supposing they can just as easily set up another. But when they find that destruction and reconstruction are not synonyms; that for the next ten years there are to be no more railroads built; no more capital coming in; no more credits given, then will they discover the mistakes they have committed, and gladly retrace their steps if they can.

With the exception of South Carolina and Georgia, nearly all the railroads of the South have been built with Northern or European capital. To construct the railroads of Virginia, that State has issued bonds to the amount of more than $35,-000,000, the greater part of which are held in the Northern States and abroad. Without such aid, her people could have hardly constructed their first road. The Missouri railroads have been constructed by the creation of a debt of nearly $30,000,000. Those of Tennessee by a State debt of some $16,000,000. The railroads of North Carolina have, with two exceptions, been built with the proceeds of State bonds. The Florida railroads have been constructed chiefly with the proceeds of her *internal improvement* bonds. The State of Louisiana has also made large issues to her railroads. The means for building the Mobile and Ohio Railroad, the great work of Alabama, were very largely drawn from England. In fact, nearly the whole Southern system has been built with the proceeds of bonds sold at the North and in Europe, not a dollar of which could have been sold with the present secession movement threatening. Virginia has only partially executed her system, and must sell $10,000,000 more bonds to complete it. North Carolina is in a similar predicament; so is South Carolina; so is Louisiana; so is Tennessee—and so are other Southern States. If the works assisted by these States must stop, how much more those based entirely upon private means or the credit of companies? For every hundred dollars that Virginia raises to-day she pays thirty, in addition to interest. If Secession be such an excellent remedy, the material salvation of the Southern States and the stepping-stone to a new era of commercial greatness and wealth, why is it that the great thermometer of public opinion, the price of their securities, is so much depressed? Why should not those of New York and Massachusetts share the same fate? If the South be as rich as is claimed, and has confidence in herself, why does she suffer her credit to be destroyed by the mere apprehensions for the future? We do not have to go far back to find quotations for Virginia Sixes at 115, forty per cent. above the present price! The same bonds *ought* to be selling to-day at 110, and would, but for Secession. So with Tennessee. The bonds of the former are selling at 74, the latter at 71. In other words, the best of all kinds of Southern property, the bonds of the Sovereign States, for which the whole means of all the people in them are in honor pledged, has lost more than 25 per cent. of its value, owing to the apprehended political action of these States.

Twenty-five per cent is too great a loss in an investment to have it repeated. But great fear exists that the excessive loss already suffered may yet be doubled or trebled. If Virginia secedes, her bonds will go to fifty cents on the dollar. In the disturbances that will certainly follow, she cannot pay the interest on them if she would. To pay it in the best of times her people have to submit to taxation which is excessive, but which must be increased more than five-fold to incur the inevitable consequences of Secession. Look at South Carolina. See what she is forced to do. Her debt is small, but if things there go on for a year as they have for three months past, she will let her interest lie over.

Such is the effect of Secession on the best investments in the South. How is it with securities of a second class— shares and bonds in railroads? These are absolutely unsaleable at almost any price; consequently all further progress of these works is brought to a dead stand. This is most unfortunate,as many of the Southern States are just in the full blow of their construction. The roads in progress, of which there are thousands of miles throughout the South, will not only be brought to a dead stand, but the traffic of those constructed will be greatly reduced. Southern disturbances will put an end to Southern travel. With the North converted into an enemy, on the ground of hostility to Southern institutions, the great mass will have to stay at home to watch and defend these institutions. Their means, instead of going into commerce, will be consumed in war, or in preparation for war. New industries cannot be developed, because these require quiet and peace. If the South can move so readily in one direction, they may with equal facility go in another. Everything permanent must have slow growth. Secession is passion, not conviction, and may, and will, be speedily turned against itself. Capital always withdraws from such a theatre as this. The madness of the movement is most astounding. Take for example Florida, with 60,000 square miles of territory, and only 87,000 white inhabitants. With desperate exertions, assisted by people at the North, she contrived to construct a railroad of 160 miles across the neck of her peninsula, with a fair promise of being able to turn over it the trade between the Eastern States and New Orleans. The road is completed, but hardly the first train has run over it. It lies almost entirely unused, and the best thing to be done with it is to strip up the rails and sell them. But for Secession it would now have been doing a good business. Northerners would have furnished the boats necessary to the *through* route. The enterprise not only might have been profitable, but worth millions to the State, so much in need of improvements and capital. Secession has put Florida back ten years. For what? A necessity that existed no where but in the minds of her political masters. The commerce of great value which was to go through her territory, enriching her people, will avoid it as a pestilence, taking the interior routes protected and rendered safe by the loyalty of the people through which they run.

SOUTHERN FREE TRADE.

One of the glories which the Southern Confederacy pictures to itself is the millenium of *free trade*. Its ideas upon this
subject were first developed by Mr. McDuffie in his famous
" forty bale" theory. They took fast hold of South Carolina,
and constitute one of the leading motives to Secession, under
which the State is to reach the very acme of wealth and
power.

One would suppose that the Cotton States enjoyed considerable freedom of trade already. All the markets of the
world are open to them. They purchase only a very small
amount of duty-paying goods in any quarter, for the reason
that there is no consumption for them among the great mass
of their population ; the whole amount directly imported into
the States from foreign countries averaging only from
$15,000,000 to $20,000,000. A considerable portion of their
imports are either on the free list or go beyond their own
limits. It is not probable that the value of foreign merchandize received by them through other ports exceeds that directly imported. The negro, who composes over one-half
of their population, consumes only American made goods.
The same may be said of a large proportion of the whites.
Three-quarters of their population, consequently, consume
no foreign merchandize worth speaking of. The greater
portion of what the rich consume also comes   from   the
North, reducing the amount of foreign, or duty-paying merchandize, to a very small fraction of the total consumption.

For at least nine-tenths of all they import, the Southern
States enjoy the most perfect freedom of trade in the cheapest and best markets for them in the world—the Northern
States. For provisions, clothing, farming utensils, furniture,
boots, shoes and hats, machinery, carriages, manufactures of
wood and iron, glass, nails, etc., etc., making up the greater
portion of what they consume, they can go nowhere else, unless they choose to pay double price for very inferior articles.
In all these they fully admit the superiority of Northern

manufactures over all the world. The Southern States consequently have, unconsciously to themselves, to be sure, been
enjoying the blessings of almost perfect freedom of trade
since the formation of the Federal Government, and under
the most favorable circumstances possible.

The only drawback to this freedom of trade in their natural
and best markets has been the slight duties paid on foreign
merchandize—say upon one-tenth of what they import. But,
by way of off-set to these duties, they have protection, a
postal service, Federal Courts and officials, the cost of maintaining all which considerably exceeds the whole revenue derived from the Southern States to the General Government
from all sources. In their new relations they do not propose
to dispense with a single one of these expenses. On the contrary, they manifest a commendable anxiety to have them all
continued and maintained. In other words, the South actually enjoy almost perfect freedom of trade, and all the advantages the Government can confer, without paying to it in
return so large a sum as is expended in their own territories
for the maintenance of the Mail Service, Courts of Justice,
and the simple administration of the Revenue Laws. Never
before were a people so fortunately placed, enjoying almost
every advantage that Government can confer, with complete
protection from foreign invasion or domestic disturbance, and
all for a less cost to themselves than the money actually dis-
bursed on their own soil.

The new era of *Free Trade* that the South propose to inaugurate is a *tax* on all they consume to support a government
which will have a double duty—defence from foreign aggression, and the confining within their own territory of the *capital*
upon which they depend for their daily bread. If Southern
independence be fairly achieved, its maintenance would have
to be constantly guaranteed by a large standing army; for it
would not do to assume the continuance of pacific terms with
the United States. If there be such a divergence between
the two as violently to part them, this mutual antipathy must
be greatly intensified after separation. In the Northern States

we are prepared to make great sacrifices for the preser-
vation of peace. The John Browns are now held in check
by ourselves. We do not allow such outrages to occur,
which are quite as injurious to our own interests as to those
of the South. We are prepared to live up to the compact,
no matter what it costs us. How will it be when we constitute two people? We shall be absolved from all *legal* obliga-
tion to protect our neighbors, and it cannot be expected that
we could, if we desired, arrest every expedition of lawless,
infatuated men. The South must protect itself against the
foes to their institutions. What would be required for such
protection? They have an exposed line of some 6,000 miles,
almost every foot of which would have to be guarded by a
strong force. Such force would have to perform two duties
—to prevent the incursion of an enemy, and the escape of
slaves, which are the capital of the South, and by which they
are now sustained. It is fearful to think that the capital of a
nation, and its almost sole means of support, and worth, as it
is rated, $4,000,000,000, is on *legs*, and may some morning
turn up *missing*. Sensible men at the South are constantly
telling their people that Secession is to bring the Canadas to
their very borders. Once in Canada the fugitive is safe, but
in no part of the Union. He does not, consequently, remain
in it. With Secession, many will find an asylum within
a mile of where they are now securely held. With a division
of the country into Free and Slave communities, a half million of soldiers would not suffice to prevent the escape of
slaves in droves. Yet the South must seek to prevent their
escape with all the force they can command.

The South, therefore, must have an immense standing army,
as a means of defence against foreign aggression, and to act
as a local police—one-half of the population being set to watch
the other. This force must be sufficient to repel any that
could be brought against it, and as the United States would,
after Secession, be a first rate military power, the seceding
States must assume to be, no matter what such assumptions
might cost.

It is also necessary to their existence that the South command the sea. All their products float upon it, and a large proportion of what they consume. To leave the highway for their products in the hands of the enemy would be quietly to resign themselves to annihilation. The United States have a powerful naval force, and in a commercial marine, equal in tonnage to that of Great Britain, and in the aptitudes of the people are capable of being a first class power on the ocean. The Southern States have neither ships nor sailors, and never can have either except by *purchase*. These things are not indigenous in their soil, and what is worse, whatever was purchased would have to be renewed every year or two, from the destructive effect of their climate on both men and materials.

How much are all these things to cost? The peace establishment of the United States, which does not contemplate the possibility of foreign aggression, comes up to some $70,000,000 annually. Can the Southern Confederated States get along with less? They have aspirations for vast foreign conquest. They must be able to match the overshadowing power of the North both upon sea and land. They must defend themselves from servile insurrections. Can all this be done for $50,000,000 annually? If so, how is this sum to be raised? It matters not much how to the Cotton States, as they have no manufacturing industries to protect. If by import duties, as now seems to be contemplated, then $50,-000,000 are to be paid in the place of $5,000,000 at the present time, and in precisely the same way. To inaugurate the principles of Free Trade the South will increase the taxes they are now paying ten-fold!

But a considerable portion of the imports of the South are food. Will the consumer consent to pay a heavy tax upon all he eats? upon the tea and coffee he drinks? upon the farming utensils he uses? in fact, upon anything that supports life, administers to his comforts, and assists his industry? And for what is he called upon to make such tremendous sacrifices? To vindicate slavery. But no one proposes to touch the institution with the weight of a finger.

THE LESSON OF THE CENSUS.

The different premises from which the North and South started necessarily lead to different results. At the enumeration following immediately upon the formation of the Government, our population was equally divided between the two sections; that of the Northern States being 1,968,455; of the Southern 1,961,372. Their respective areas were 166,358 square miles for the Northern States, and 296,345 for the Southern. At the last enumeration the area of the Northern States had increased to 847,816 miles; of the Southern to 888,310. Their population had advanced to 19,139,194, or at the rate of about 875 per cent, for the Northern States and Territories, and to 12,509,644, or about 542 per cent. for the Southern.

The rate of this increase, from decade to decade, will be seen in the following table:

DECADES.	POPULATION NORTHERN STATES.	POPULATION SOUTHERN STATES.	EXCESS IN NORTHERN STATES.
1790	1,968,455	1,961,372	7,083
1800	2,683,652	2,621,296	62,356
1810	3,738,065	3,501,749	236,316
1820	5,152,292	4,485,839	666,453
1830	7,018,627	5,848,293	1,170,334
1840	9,728,922	7,334,431	2,394,491
1850	13,527,220	9,654,656	3,872,564
1860	19,139,194	12,509,644	6,629,550

Never was a race commenced with parties more equally matched. They were equal in numbers. In resources the Southern States appeared to have the advantage. As their people expanded, further room was secured by the purchase of Louisiana and Florida. For the first thirty years the two sections were neck and neck, when the North, taught by the war of 1812, began to turn their attention to manufacturing and to the employment of those agencies upon which the creation of wealth, and at the same time of population, depends. So long as both sections devoted themselves to agriculture, their increase was very nearly equal. But the North, not content with this alone, took a new line of industry in

which the South could not follow, because they would not
train their workmen to anything but the rudest kind of labor.
They were consequently distanced long ago. Within the last
decade the North increased at the rate of 41 per cent. on a
population of 13,527,220; the South 29 per cent. on a population of 9,654,656. At the same ratio of increase the North,
in 1870, will have 26,976,273 inhabitants; the South 16,537,-
440. In 1880 the North will have 38,050,744; the South
21,333,297. In one hundred years from the first enumeration
the North will have 53,661,549, and the South 27,519,953.
In other words, in the first one hundred years from the organization of the Government, the North, by the superiority
of its industry, will have increased its population at a rate
equaling twice that of the Southern States.

With numbers go wealth and power; with twice the population of the South, the North will be five times as rich and
strong. The South see this colossal development, and try to
escape by dissolving the Union—in other words, by provok-
ing its hostility instead of availing themselves of its strength;
and by taking a course that must increase instead of remov-
ing the disparity. The North is not to blame for its strength,
but they well know that as all this has been gained by arts
of peace, a great deal of it may be lost by war. Hence the
striking contrast between the conduct of the two sections.
In the South it is war, war! The whole country, if possible,
is to be converted into a military camp. In the North we are
seeking to conserve our material interests, to maintain uninterrupted the channels of internal communication, to keep
our laborers employed, and maintain unchecked our marvelous progress. In case of collision indifferent parties see but
one issue—the overwhelming triumph of the North. We
have authority for such a conclusion in our vast superiority in
whatever can give strength. We hold uninterupted command
of the sea, and in a year's time could, if we chose, without
any other sacrifice than the loss of trade, reduce every offend-
ing State to beggary. Yet we are as loath to assume the
offensive as if we were the weakest people in the world. We

cannot get rid of the idea that the Southern people are still brethren, whose blood we must not shed. We are unconscious of offence, and consequently cherish no sentiments of hostility or revenge. We extend the same welcome to Southern people that we ever did. We will not allow that the repeated acts of official and individual treachery express the prevailing sentiment at the South. We forbear, conscious of our rectitude and our strength. But, more than all, we shrink from the thought of destroying, with our own hands, the fair fabric we had erected, so long the hope for mankind, founded upon the idea that left free, the better part of man's nature would mould his institutions and guide his conduct. We have at the North, at least, felt our mission to be the most sacred that could be committed to a people. We consequently tolerate and excuse many things to preserve the great principle. The most degraded and ignorant foreigner as soon, almost, as he lands on our shores, we declare to be a man, and receive him into full citizenship. We respect his manhood, not his accidents. By making war upon our brother, shall we proclaim to the world the failure of our grand experiment, and confess that brute force must still continue to mark the relations between man and man, and government and subject ?

It is natural that the South should view with apprehension the rapidly expanding power of the North, which they can no longer hope to rival. But they entirely misinterpret the sentiment of their people, who, being devoted to the arts of peace, dread everything like sudden change. It is natural that the North should have rallied almost unanimously to put down the administration of Mr. Buchanan, as profligate and corrupt as any in history. Had the people been no better, society itself must have come to an end. But that the change did not mean a hostile interference with Southern institutions is fully proved by the entire inaction of the North, now that power is fully secured. With the subject of slavery the North do not desire to become implicated. They know not how to deal with it if they desired. They prefer to ignore the whole matter. At the same time we cannot apostrophise the institution as we do those of freedom, because we trace to the latter our own strength, and to the former the weakness of the South. In idea we estimate values by results, and consequently speak of freedom as better than slavery. Notwithstanding the disparity, the South is safe only in the Union. In it the changes that take place must be natural, having all the health and appearance of growth. In this way any step that helps to make Virginia a Free State is mutually beneficial to North and South. The latter wants more labor; the former more room. When Virginia is free, similar influences will begin to work in North Carolina, but no faster than they promote the general good. The whole thing will be left to popular election. When a person in Virginia fancies he can make more money by the use of free labor than slave, or steam than muscular power, he will do so, sending off his slaves and bring five times, probably, as many free people to fill their place. Virginia has such vast resources that can only be properly developed by free labor, that the substitution of one for the other will soon become rapid. Are not all to be benefited by such changes? If so, why not await the action of time, which is always beneficent, instead of resorting to violence, which is always destruction.

Population increases in ratio to the means provided for its support—in other words, in ratio to intelligence. The blacks, South, consequently, increase more slowly than the whites.

The ratio of this increase will be seen in the following statement:

YEARS.	TOTAL NUMBER OF SLAVES.	INCREASE IN EACH TEN YEARS.	RATE OF INCREASE.
1790..................	697,697	......	....
1800..................	893,041	195,144	27.9
1810..................	1,191,364	298,323	33.4
1820..................	1,538,038	346,674	29.0
1830..................	2,009,043	471,005	30.6
1840..................	2,487,455	478,412	23.8
1850..................	3,200,364	716,858	28.8
1860..................	3,999,313	798,949	25.0

The rate of increase of whites in the Slaveholding States and Territories since the formation of the Government has been as follows:

YEARS.	TOTAL NUMBER.	INCREASE EACH TEN YEARS.	RATE OF INCREASE.
1790	1,271,488	......	...
1800	1,702,980	431,492	33.9
1810	2,208,785	505,805	29.7
1820	2,831,560	622,775	28.2
1830	3,662,606	831,046	29.3
1840	4,809,097	1,146,491	26.5
1850	6,412,605	1,603,508	34.2
1860	8,435,020	2,022,415	31.3

The ratio of increase in the Free States and Territories has been as follows:

YEARS.	TOTAL NUMBER.	INCREASE EACH TEN YEARS.	PER CENTAGE OF INCREASE.
1790	1,968,455	......	....
1800	2,683,652	715,197	36.8
1810	3,738,065	1,054,413	40.4
1820	5,152,292	1,414,227	37.7
1830	7,018,627	1,866,335	36.6
1840	9,728,922	2,710,295	39.1
1850	13,527,220	3,798,298	39.4
1860	19,139,194	5,611,974	41.0

This ratio of increase in favor of the North is constantly becoming greater from the gradual movement of the black population southward. Delaware is virtually a Free State. Missouri having less than ten per cent. of her population slaves, must also rank in a very few years with the Free States. One half of Virginia, an area of 30,000 square miles, contains only 22,000 slaves. A third of Kentucky only about 7,000. Three-eights of Tennessee only about 25,000. In all these slaves are decreasing instead of increasing, and their places must soon be taken by a population entirely free.

On the succeeding pages we have given the results of the Census of 1860, as far as they have been published, compared with the Census of 1840 and 1850.

STATEMENT *showing the Area of the several States and Territories, with the number of Inhabitants in each in 1840, 1850 and 1860:*

STATES AND TERRITORIES.	Area in Sq. Miles.	NUMBER OF INHABITANTS.		
		1840.	1850.	1860.
Free States.				
Maine	31,766	501,793	583,169	619,958
New Hampshire	9,280	284,574	317,976	327,072
Vermont	10,212	291,948	314,120	315,827
Massachusetts	7,800	737,699	994,514	1,231,494
Rhode Island	1,306	108,830	147,545	174,621
Connecticut	4,674	309,978	370,792	460,670
New York	47,000	2,428,921	3,097,394	3,851,561
New Jersey	8,320	373,306	489,555	676,084
Pennsylvania	46,000	1,724,033	2,311,786	2,916,018
Ohio	39,964	1,519,467	1,980,329	2.377,917
Indiana	33,809	685,866	988,416	1,350,802
Michigan	56,451	212,267	397,654	754,291
Illinois	55,410	476,183	851,470	1,691,238
Wisconsin	53,924	30,945	305,391	768,495
Iowa	55,045	43,112	192,214	682,002
Minnesota	95,274	....	6,077	172,793
Oregon	102,500	....	13,294	52,566
California	188,981	....	92,597	364,770
Kansas	125,293	....	....	143,645
Total Free States	847,816	9,728,922	13,454,293	18,951,814
Slave States.				
Delaware	2,120	78.085	91,532	112,353
Maryland	11,124	470,019	583,034	731,965
Virginia	61,352	1,239,797	1,421,661	1,593,199
North Carolina	50,704	753,419	669,039	1,008,342
South Carolina	29,785	594,398	668,507	715,371
Georgia	58,000	691,392	906,185	1,052,757
Florida	59,268	54,477	87,445	154,694
Alabama	50,722	590,756	771,623	955,917
Mississippi	47,156	375,651	606,526	887,158
Louisiana	41,255	352,411	517,762	666,431
Texas	274,366	....	212,592	600,955
Arkansas	52,198	97,574	209,897	440,775
Missouri	67,380	383,702	682,044	1,201,209
Kentucky	37,680	779,828	982,405	1,145,567
Tennessee	45,600	829,210	1,002,717	1,146,640
Total Slave States	898,310	7,290,719	9 612,969	12,434,373
Territories.				
Nebraska	293,438	....	....	28,893
Dakotah	60,000	....	....	4,839
Washington	223,022	....	....	11,624
Utah	269,170	....	11,380	60,000
New Mexico	256,309	....	61,547	92,024
Indian	71,127	....	....	....
Total Territories	1,163,066	....	72,927	187,390
District of Columbia	60	43,712	51,687	75,321
Grand total of United States	3,024,535	17,063,353	23,191,876	31,649,688

64   POPULATION OF THE UNITED STATES.

STATEMENT *showing the Absolute Increase of Population of each State and Territory for the last three decades, with the per cent. of such increase.*

STATES AND TERRITORIES.	DECENNIAL INCREASE.					
	Absolute.			Per Centage.		
	1830-40.	1840-50.	1850-60.	'30-'40	'40-'50	'50-'60
Free States.						
Maine	102,338	81,376	36,789	25 62	16 22	6.31
New Hampshire	15,246	33,402	9,096	5.66	11.74	2.86
Vermont	11,296	22,172	1,707	4.02	7.59	0.54
Massachusetts	127,291	256,615	336,980	20 83	34.81	23.99
Rhode Island	11,631	38,715	27,076	11.97	35.57	18.35
Connecticut	12,303	60,814	89,878	4.13	19.62	24.23
New York	510,313	668,473	754,167	26.60	27.52	24.35
New Jersey	52,483	116,249	186,529	16.35	31.14	38.10
Pennsylvania	375,800	587,753	604,232	27.87	34.09	26.13
Ohio	581,564	460,862	397,598	62.01	30.33	20.08
Indiana	342,835	302,550	362,386	99.94	44.11	36.57
Michigan	180,628	185,387	356,637	570.90	87.34	89.66
Illinois	318,738	375,287	839,768	202.44	78.81	98.62
Wisconsin	30,945	274,446	463,094	....	886.88	151 68
Iowa	43,112	149,102	489,788	....	345.85	254.81
Minnesota	....	6,077	156,716	....	....	274.34
Oregon	....	13,294	39,272	....	....	294.73
California	....	92,597	292,173	....	....	151.90
Kansas	....	....	143,645	....	....	....
Total Free States	2,716,523	3,725,371	5,497,521	38.65	33.29	40.88
Slave States.						
Delaware	1,337	13,447	20,821	1.74	17.22	22.74
Maryland	22,979	113,015	146,931	5 14	24.04	25 44
Virginia	28,392	181,564	171,538	2.34	14.67	12.05
North Carolina	15,432	115,620	139,303	2.09	15.35	16.03
South Carolina	13,213	74,109	46,864	2.27	12,47	6.01
Georgia	174,569	214,793	176,612	33.78	31.07	19.49
Florida	19,747	32,968	59,249	56.86	60.52	66.61
Alabama	281,229	180,867	184,294	90.86	30.62	23.89
Mississippi	239,030	230,875	280,632	174.96	61.46	46.31
Louisiana	136,672	165,351	148,669	63.35	46.92	28.71
Texas	....	212,592	388,363	....	....	182.63
Arkansas	67,186	112,323	230,878	221.09	115.12	109.94
Missouri	243,247	298,342	519,165	173 18	77.75	76.12
Kentucky	91,911	202,577	163,162	13.36	25.98	16.62
Tennessee	147,306	173,507	143,923	24 60	20.92	14.34
Total Slave States	1,482,251	2,322,250	2,821,404	25.52	31.95	29.35
Territories.						
Nebraska	....	....	28,893	....	....	....
Dakotah	....	....	4,839	....	....	....
Washington	....	....	11,624	....	....	....
Utah	....	....	38,620	....	....	239.37
New Mexico	....	....	30,477	....	....	49.52
Indian	....	....	....	....	....	....
Total Territories	....	....	114,453	....	....	156.79
District of Columbia	3,878	7,975	23,634	9.74	18 25	45 45
Grand total	4,202,651	6,028,523	8,457,012	32 67	35 87	36 46

STATEMENT *showing the per centage of Slaves in each State, the Population to the square mile, and the number of Representatives for each.*

STATES AND TERRITORIES	PER CENT. OF SLAVES TO POPULATION.			RATIO OF POPULATION TO SQUARE MILE.			REPRESN'TIVES IN CONGRESS.		
	1840.	1850.	1860.	1840.	1850.	1860.	1840	1850	1860
Free States.									
Maine	....	....	....	15.80	18.36	19.52	7	6	5
New Hampshire	....	....	....	30.67	34.26	35 22	4	3	3
Vermont	....	....	....	28.59	30.92	30 92	4	3	2
Massachusetts	....	....	....	94.58	127 50	170 70	10	11	10
Rhode Island	....	....	....	83.33	112.97	133.71	2	2	1
Connecticut	....	....	....	66.32	79.33	98.86	4	4	4
New York	....	....	....	51.68	65.90	81.98	34	33	30
New Jersey	0.18	0.05	....	44.67	58 64	81.27	5	5	5
Pennsylvania	0.01	....	....	37.46	50 26	63.39	24	25	23
Ohio	....	....	....	38.02	49.55	59.45	21	21	19
Indiana	....	....	....	20 23	29 24	39.69	10	11	11
Michigan	....	....	....	3.77	7 07	13.39	3	4	6
Illinois	0 07	....	....	8 59	15.37	30.53	7	9	13
Wisconsin	....	....	....	0.57	5.66	14 26	..	3	6
Iowa	....	....	....	0.78	3.48	12.39	..	2	5
Minnesota	....	....	....	....	0.06	1.81	..	..	1
Oregon	....	....	....	....	0.13	0.52	..	..	1
California	....	....	....	....	0.49	2 04	..	2	3
Kansas	....	....	....	....	....	1.14	..	..	1
Total Free States	....	....	....	11.47	15 87	22.34	135	144	149
Slave States.									
Delaware	3,34	2.50	1.66	36.83	43.18	52.99	1	1	1
Maryland	19.11	15.50	11.67	42.25	52.41	61.29	6	6	6
Virginia	36.22	33.24	31 12	20.21	23.17	25 92	15	13	11
North Carolina	32.63	33 20	32.56	14 85	17.14	21.39	9	8	7
South Carolina	55.02	57.59	56.92	20 23	22.75	24.31	7	6	4
Georgia	40.64	42.13	43.17	11.65	15.62	18 68	8	8	7
Florida	47.21	44.96	43.79	0 92	1.48	2 48	..	1	1
Alabama	42.92	44 43	45.55	11.93	15.21	18.78	7	7	6
Mississippi	51 89	51.07	54 06	7 97	12.86	19.58	4	5	5
Louisiana	47.81	47.23	46.84	8.54	12,55	16.13	4	4	4
Texas	....	27.33	30.94	....	0.78	2 19	..	2	4
Arkansas	42.95	44.52	24.74	1.87	4.02	8.44	1	2	3
Missouri	15.13	12.84	9.62	5 69	10 12	17.82	5	7	9
Kentucky	23.35	21.39	19.48	20.70	26.07	30.39	10	10	8
Tennessee	22.03	23.81	25.03	18.16	21.99	25.19	11	10	8
Total Slave States	34.03	33.29	32.16	8.21	10.82	13 91	88	90	84
Territories.									
Nebraska	....	....	....	....	....	0.10	..	..	..
Dakotah	....	....	....	....	....	0.08	..	..	..
Washington	....	....	....	....	....	0.05	..	..	..
Utah	....	0 01	....	....	0.04	0.19	..	..	..
New Mexico	....	....	....	....	0.24	0.36	..	..	..
Indian	....	....	....	....	....	....	..	..	..
Total Territories	....	....	....	....	0.05	0.16	..	..	..
District of Columbia	10.71	7.12	5.83	473 12	661 45	1255.42	..	..	..
Grand total	14.58	13 81	12 64	5.64	7.67	10 46	223	234	233

THE GEOGRAPHICAL QUESTION OF SECESSION.

The attempt of the Cotton States to divide the country upon the line between free and slaveholding territory, has signally failed. In large portions of every State in which slaves are held, they are not the paramount interest. In such the conviction is universal that they must, ere long, give way to labor better adapted to their soil and climate, and to the development of their resources. In all such districts, consequently, we find loyalty to government, and sympathy with the North.

This want of homogeneousness has already divided the people of the Southern States into two hostile camps. It is the South seceding from the South, showing a confederacy co-extensive with territory in which slaves are held to be impossible. In more than one-half of this territory, the staple, for the cultivation of which slave labor is considered necessary, cannot be grown. Where they cannot, its industries are identical with those of 'the Northern States. It has the climate of the North, from its great elevation above the sea. Upon it the slave comprises only a small fraction of the population. If we start from the southwest corner of Maryland, and follow, to the southern boundary of Virginia, the ridge separating the waters flowing into the Ohio from those flowing into the Atlantic, we shall divide the State into nearly equal parts. Continued southward in the same general direction, we include mountainous portions of North Carolina and Georgia, and following the west in direction of the Alleghany range, the northern portion of Alabama. The western boundary of this territory would include one-third of Kentucky and three-eighths of Tennessee, the whole embracing about 75,000 square miles, forming a compact and contiguous mass. It has a width, from east to west, of over two hundred miles, and a length, from north to south, of over four hundred, and embraces the whole elevated plain from which the Alleghenies rise. It presents similar topographical and climatic features for its entire extent.

The population of this territory, by counties, free and slave, according to the census of 1850 was as follows:

VIRGINIA.

COUNTIES.	TOTAL POPULATION.	NUMBER OF SLAVES.	COUNTIES.	TOTAL POPULATION.	NUMBER OF SLAVES.
Barbour····	9,005	113	Monroe····	10,204	1,061
Boone······	3,237	183	Nicholas····	3,963	73
Braxton····	4,212	89	Ohio········	18,066	164
Brooke·····	5,054	31	Pocahontas ·	3,598	267
Cabell······	5,299	389	Preston·····	11,708	87
Carroll·····	5,409	154	Pulaski·····	5,118	1,471
Dodridge····	2,750	32	Putnam·····	5,338	632
Fayette ····	3,955	156	Raleigh ····	1,765	23
Floyd.······	6,458	443	Randolph···	5,243	201
Giles·······	6,570	657	Ritchie·····	3,902	16
Gilmer·····	3,475	72	Russell·····	11,919	982
Grayson ····	6,677	499	Scott·······	9,829	473
Greenbrier··	10,022	1,317	Smythe·····	8,162	1,064
Hancock····	4,050	3	Taylor·····	5,367	168
Harrison····	11,728	488	Tazwell ····	9,942	1,060
Jackson ····	6,544	53	Tyler.······	5,498	38
Kahnawa ···	15,353	3,140	Washington·	14,612	2,131
Lee·······	10,267	787	Wayne.·····	4,760	189
Lewis······	10,131	368	Wetzell····	4,284	17
Logan······	3,620	87	Wirt.·······	3,353	32
Marion.·····	10,552	94	Wood.······	9,450	373
Marshall···	10,138	49	Wyoming···	1,645	61
Mason······	7,539	647	Wythe·····	12,024	2,185
Mercer.·····	4,222	177			
Monongalia ·	12,387	176	Total·····	339,404	22,912

TENNESSEE.

COUNTIES.	TOTAL POPULATION.	NUMBER OF SLAVES.	COUNTIES.	TOTAL POPULATION.	NUMBER OF SLAVES.
Anderson ···	6,938	506	McMinn ····	13,906	1,564
Bledsoe·····	5,959	827	Marion·····	6,314	551
Blount ·····	12,424	1,084	Meigs······	4,879	395
Bradley ····	12,259	744	Monroe·····	11,874	1,189
Campbell ···	6,068	918	Morgan·····	3,430	101
Carter······	6,296	353	Overton·····	11,211	1,065
Clarborne···	9,369	660	Polk·······	6,338	400
Cooke···· ··	8,310	719	Rhea ·······	4,415	436
Fentress ····	4,464	148	Roane······	12,185	1,544
Grainger····	12,370	1,035	Scott·······	1,905	37
Greene·····	17,824	1,093	Sevier······	6,920	403
Hamilton ···	10,075	672	Sullivan····	11,742	1,004
Hancock····	5,660	202	Van Buren.·	2,674	175
Hawkins····	13,371	1,690	Washington ·	13,861	930
Jackson ····	15,673	1,558	White······	11,444	1,214
Jefferson ·· ·	13,204	1,628			
Johnson.····	3,705	206			
Knox·······	18,807	2,193	Total·····	306,874	27,243

KENTUCKY.

COUNTIES.	TOTAL POPULATION.	NUMBER OF SLAVES.	COUNTIES.	TOTAL POPULATION.	NUMBER OF SLAVES.
Breathitt····	3,795	170	Letcher·····	2,512	62
Carter······	6,241	257	Lewis·· ····	7,202	322
Clay·· ·····	5,421	515	Morgan·····	7,620	187
Clinton ·····	4,889	262	Owsley······	3,774	136
Estill·······	5,785	411	Perry ······	3,092	117
Floyd·· ····	5,714	149	Pike··· ····	5,365	98
Greenup····	9,654	606	Pulaski·····	14,195	1,307
Harlan·· ····	4,268	123	Rockcastle ··	4,697	375
Johnson ····	3,873	30	Wayne ·····	8,692	830
Knox·······	7,050	612	Whitley·····	7,447	201
Laurell·····	4,445	192			
Lawrence····	6,281	137	Total·····	132,002	7,099

NORTH CAROLINA.

COUNTIES.	TOTAL POPULATION.	NUMBER OF SLAVES.	COUNTIES.	TOTAL POPULATION.	NUMBER OF SLAVES.
Alexander ··	5,220	543	Henderson ··	6,853	924
Ashe··· ····	8,777	595	McDowal.···	6,246	1,262
Burke·· ····	7,772	2,132	Macon·······	6,389	549
Buncombe ··	13,425	1,717	Rutherford ··	13,550	2,905
Caldwell····	6,317	1,203	Watauga..···	3,400	129
Catawba····	8,862	1,569	Wilkes·· ···	12,099	1,142
Cherokee.···	6,838	337	Yancy······	8,205	346
Cleveland···	10,396	1,747			
Heywood.···	7,074	418	Total·····	131,023	17,518

GEORGIA

COUNTIES.	TOTAL POPULATION.	NUMBER OF SLAVES.	COUNTIES.	TOTAL POPULATION.	NUMBER OF SLAVES.
Cass········	13,300	3,008	Lumpkin ···	8,955	939
Chatoga.····	6,815	1,680	Murray·····	14,433	1,930
Cherokee·.··	12,800	1,157	Paulding· ··	7,039	1,377
Floyd··· ···	8,205	2,999	Rabun·· ····	2,448	110
Forsythe.· ··	8,550	1,027	Walker·····	13,109	1,664
Gilmer··· ··	8,440	200			
Gordon·· ····	5,984	828			
Habersham.·	8,895	1,218	Total·····	118,973	18,137

ALABAMA.

COUNTIES.	TOTAL POPULATION.	NUMBER OF SLAVES.	COUNTIES.	TOTAL POPULATION.	NUMBER OF SLAVES.
Blount······	7,367	426	Randolph···	11,584	1,321
Cherokee· ··	13,884	1,691	St. Clair····	6,829	266
Hancock····	1,542	62	Walker·····	5,124	936
Lawrence· ··	14,088	2,292			
Marion.·····	7,833	908			
Marshall····	8,846	868	Total·····	77,097	8,770

The whole territory described, which forms a compact and contiguous body, contained, in 1850, a population of 1,105,-313, of whom 101,079, or 9 per cent. only, were slaves. We have not the returns, by counties, for 1860, but the rate of increase of the white population for the past ten years must have been equal to 20 per cent., while that of slaves must have remained very nearly stationary. At the present moment this great district must have a population of 1,300,000, of whom not over eight per cent, or 104,000, are slaves. It has an excellent climate, probably the best in the United States. Much of it is elevated from 2,000 to 3,000 feet above the sea, and is admirably adapted to grazing and the cultivation of the grains, while beneath the soil is the greatest profusion of the most valuable minerals. Upon no portion of it can cotton be successfully cultivated, nor the slaves profitably employed. Though at present thinly settled, it is capable of a much denser population than any portions of the States of which it forms a part, and is only wanting in means of intercommunication, which are now being supplied, to render it the most attractive field for emigration and industry in the United States. Its people, in their habits, ideas and interests, as well as in the physical features of their country, present contrasts to the cotton districts as striking as exists between these and the North. They control the Secession movement in Virginia, North Carolina and Tennessee, and would control it in Georgia and Alabama could they have been permitted to vote upon it, as were those of Tennessee and North Carolina. They will no more submit to the dictation of the Montgomery oligarchs than New York or Pennsylvania. Their interests are more directly opposed than those between the Cotton States and the extreme North, because the wide distance that separates the latter renders them independent of each other, while the Cotton States are seeking, by every possible means, to drag all the Slave States with them, for the purpose of compelling them to share their burdens, and of giving greater strength and dignity to their cause.

This great tongue or wedge of land carries Northern ideas,

Northern industry, and Northern population right into the heart of Cottondom, and within two hundred miles of the Gulf of Mexico. It is now, and must continue to be, the stratagetical line controlling the whole question of Secession. It now holds the Border States. Should Eastern Virginia go, Western Virginia would not. If Western Tennessee should, the Eastern portion of the State would not. They are very well satisfied with things as they are. They do not propose to cultivate cotton fields; but to grow grain, raise stock and work minerals, and in time to become a great manufacturing people. They are not going to submit to enormous taxes for the benefit of slave propogandism. They tolerate slavery, but want no more, and soon hope to get rid of the the few slaves they have.

The accompanying map illustrates, in a striking manner, the relation of this territory to the question of Secession. The figures upon it show the ratio of the slave to the white population, which is also shown by the different degrees of shade. The territory upon which the slave does not exceed one-tenth of the population is left white. Where the population is so small its protection and development can never guide the legislation of a State. Where such territory is contiguous, so that its inhabitants can sustain and support each other, they are not be overawed or driven in any direction adverse to their interest.

Here, then, is a standing menace to Southern Confederacy, within sight of their own capitol, and quite competent to break the back of Secession without any aid from the North. But suppose the General Government were disposed to aid it, and should do so by offering to purchase every slave within this 75,000 square miles of territory? For this, $50,000,000 would be ample. It would be the best investment ever made by a nation. At present these 100,000 slaves block the way to millions of freemen. Nearly every one of them are unprofitable; yet they are so interwoven with the white population, as heir-looms and family servants, that they only slowly disappear. Plant a million of mechanics and artisans in their places, and the profits of their industry would be greater than that of all the slaves in the United States. The Cotton States are even more interested than the Northern in making this territory free, as a means of obtaining abundance of food, manufactures of iron, agricultural and domestic implements of all kinds, at the cheapest rates, and almost at their doors, and of enlarging, at the same time, the market for their great staples.

The map also illustrates the impossibility of dividing the country upon any *political* boundary. These are accidental, and produce no corresponding change in the habits and character of the inhabitants living upon them. If the Cotton States would obtain peace, after their fashion, they must have uniformity, by excluding all elements of disturbance, and all territory better adapted to free labor than to slave. But this would leave their own so reduced in area, and so cut to pieces by hostile and stratagetical lines as to be entirely inadequate for the foundation of a new Nationality, which must immediately come in conflict with a first class power, or maintain such an attitude as will involve the expenditures of a first class power. It would leave a majority of the Cotton States shorn of one half of their domains. The disaffected portions should be got rid of as soon as possible. With these would be lost all that portion of the population which, from its climate and pursuits, contained any real strength. The new Confederacy, reduced to the area of the planting districts, would have plenty to attend to without the pastime of forming new Empires. With one-half of its numbers slaves; with a discontented population of whites, who do not in the Cotton districts, as elsewhere, from their industry and intelligence, constitute the real strength of the nation; and without the means of realizing a single one of its aims, it will not be long before every member of it will heartily wish himself back in the bosom of the *Old* Confederacy, which gave both dignity and protection at the lowest possible cost, and which allowed every reasonable scope to individual action, tolerated every kind of opinion, and made obedience to

law, within its limited sphere, the only test of nationality. To
the bosom of this Confederacy all must in time return, no
matter how eccentric may be the present action of the refac-
tory members. They have embarked in a contest in which
natural laws, and the public and private welfare are against
them. Such a contest cannot be long sustained. The excessive burdens which the people of the new Confederacy will
soon be called on to bear, will be contrasted with the millenium of protection, quiet and prosperity enjoyed under the
Federal Government, and which can never be regained but
under the banner which has signalized our triumphs, and is
the symbol of our unity.

www.ingramcontent.com/pod-product-compliance
Lightning Source LLC
Chambersburg PA
CBHW020241090426
42735CB00010B/1787